Dark Psychology: How to Analyze People

Learn the secrets of the human mind manipulation against deception and brainwashing through this beginner's guide. Discover the art of influence people through persuasion, NLP, and emotional intelligence.

BY

Chris Cooper

information is without contract or any type of guarantee assurance.

The trademarks that are used are without any consent, and the publication of the trademark is without permission or backing by the trademark owner. All trademarks and brands within this book are for clarifying purposes only and are the owned by the owners themselves, not affiliated with this document.

Table of contents

Part 1: Dark Psychology

Part 2: How to Analyze People

Part 1 : Dark Psychology

Introduction

Dark Psychology is the act of manipulating and controlling the mind. The most potent persuaders use it. Narcissism, Machiavellianism, and psychopathy are considered the main components of Dark Psychology. It's a fact that every human has the potential to victimize others or becoming a victim of others. These days' people use love bombing, involve others, get their purpose, and leave. Persuasion is now different from the past, and it has become part of everyday life. Many of us are using persuasion or coercion to get their goal achieved. From public speakers, politicians, leaders to advertisements, different convincing methods are applied for controlling minds. There may be the use of appeal to reason or request to emotion technique for getting the attention. If you are persuading for something, remember it's the purpose that matters. For a better influence, you can adopt some strategies such as persistence, active listening ability, good reputation, excellent communication skills, but always remembering that persuasion is not manipulation. It is because manipulation causes many mental disorders, including Borderline Personality Disorder and Narcissistic Personality Disorder. One can observe distinct signs of manipulation, including passive-aggressive behavior, implicit threats, dishonesty, gas lighting, or verbal abuse. The manipulators involve you in intellectual as well as bureaucratic bullying. They never accept responsibility for their mistakes and always criticize you by using your feelings against you. But, there are some ways to avoid manipulative people in your life as showing disengagement, staying focused on the subject, and by tackling the situation by addressing manipulation in a therapy. You should know your fundamental human rights.

Brainwashing and hypnosis terms are also used in controlling one's mind and getting the desired target. In brainwashing, cults may use sleep deprivation, isolation, guilt, or self-betrayal to change one's mentality. Neuro-linguistic programing in Dark Psychology is the best way ensuring you that how you can get what you want and how to take work out of people by controlling their minds. In this technique, the use of non-verbal communication brings a positive transition in your decision making. A significant word emotional intelligence is known to most of us has a lot of impact on one's life. It contributes even more to tackle a situation than intellectual equity. So, using tips to increase emotional intelligence will be helpful. Use emotional intelligence and control your thoughts. Moreover, Case studies from past will also valuable to get a lesson.

Chapter 1: Basics of Dark Psychology

Dark psychology is the study of a person's mind as it applies to people's psychological intent of preying on others. Humanity, as a whole, has this capacity to victimize other human beings and life forms. This urge is restrained or sublimated by many, some act upon these urges. Dark Psychology seeks to understand the emotions, feelings, and beliefs that contribute to the actions of human predators. Dark Psychology believes that development is purposive, and 99.99 percent of the time has some logical, goal-oriented motivation. Under Dark Psychology, the remaining.01 percent is the violent victimization of others without purposeful intent or somewhat defined by evolutionary psychology or religious doctrine.

1.1 Narcissism

Narcissism is not just something that's ascribed to people posting selfies and listing all their favorite Facebook meals. It's a diagnosable personality disorder that causes a delusional sense of self-worth and a lack of empathy in people.
Do you know someone who deserves endless praise, who thinks they are better than anyone else, but at the slightest criticism, flies off the handle? Such tips will help you find a narcissist and deal with him.

Narcissistic Personality Disorder

In our self-obsessed, celebrity-driven culture, the word narcissism gets tossed around a lot, often to describe someone who seems excessively arrogant or full of himself. Yet narcissism doesn't mean self-love in psychological terms— at least not of a severe nature. We can say that people with narcissistic personality disorder are in love with an idealized, bombastic self-image that is more accurate. And they are in love with that inflated self-image precisely because it helps them to escape intense anxiety feelings. But it takes a lot of work to prop up their delusions of adequacy— and that's where the unhealthy attitudes and behaviors come in.

Narcissistic personality disorder includes a pattern of ego-centered, narcissistic thought and behavior, a lack of compassion and concern for others, and an overwhelming admiration need. Some also characterize the NPD as cocky, arrogant, greedy, condescending, and demanding. This way of thinking and acting appears in all aspects of the narcissist's life: from work and friendships to relationships with family and love.

Those with narcissistic personality disorder are highly resistant to change their behavior, even if it causes problems for them. A propensity is to blame other people. What's more, they're susceptible, and they react badly to even the slightest criticism, disagreement, or perceived slights they see as a personal attack. It's often more comfortable for the people in the life of the narcissist to go along with their requests and escape the coldness and rages. Nonetheless, you will identify the narcissists in your life through learning more about the narcissistic personality disorder, shielding yourself from their power plays, and setting healthy limits.

Signs of Narcissistic Personality Disorder

- **Grandiosity- A Sense of Self-importance**

Grandiosity is the hallmark of narcissism. Grandiosity is not just pride or arrogance but an excessive sense of superiority. Narcissists feel they are unique or "special" and only other extraordinary people can understand them. What's more, they're too perfect for anything standard or normal. We want to associate with and be associated with other high-status people, places, and things. Narcissists always think they're better than everyone else and deserve praise as such — even if they've done nothing to earn it. We will often exaggerate their successes and strengths, or lie outright about them. And when they're talking about jobs or relationships, all you'll hear is how much they're doing, how nice they are, and how grateful the people are to have them in their lives. They're the undisputed champion, and everybody else is a bit of a player at best.

- **A Narcissistic Person Lives in Imagination World that Supports his Delusions of Grandeur**

Because reality does not help the grandiose vision of itself, narcissists live in a world of illusion assisted by exaggeration, self-deception, and superstition. They spin self-glorifying fantasies that make them feel unique and in charge of limitless achievement, strength, creativity, beauty, and ideal love. Such fantasies shield them from feelings of inner loneliness and guilt, so they disregard or rationalize facts and opinions which contradict them. Anything which attempts to burst the bubble of delusion is met with extreme defensiveness and even anger.

It is so that those around the narcissist learn to treat their denial of reality carefully.

- ## Narcissist Wants Constant Admiration and Praise

The sense of superiority of a narcissist is like a balloon that slowly loses air without a firm stream of applause and recognition to put it swollen. The occasional praise is not appropriate. Narcissists need consistent food for their ego, so they are surrounded by people eager to respond to their excessive need for approval. Such partnerships are very unilateral. It's all about what the narcissist admirer can do, never the other way around. And if the admirer's devotion so appreciation is ever disrupted or reduced, the narcissist views it as treason.

- ## They have Sense of Entitlement

Narcissists expect favorable treatment as their right since they consider themselves different. They genuinely believe they should be getting whatever they want. They always understand the people around them to honor their every wish and desire automatically. That is just their interest. If you don't predict their every need and fulfill them, then you're useless. And if you have the nerve to question their will or ask for something "selfishly" in exchange, brace yourself for violence, anger, or cold shoulder.

- **They Exploit without Shame and Guilt**

Narcissists never develop the ability to connect with other people's feelings–to place themselves in the shoes of others. Or put it another way, they lack empathy. In many ways, they see the people as objects in their lives — around to serve their needs. Consequently, they do not think twice about taking advantage of others to reach their ends. Such behavioral manipulation is sometimes malicious, but it is often actually insensitive. Narcissists don't think about how others affect their behavior. And if you find that out, they're still not going to get it. They only understand their own needs.

- **They Frequently Demean, Intimidate, Bullies, and Belittle to Others**

Narcissists feel intimidated every time they come across someone who seems to have something they lack — especially those who are confident and famous. Those who don't bow down them or who criticize them in any way are challenging them too. The mode of defense is hate. The only way to neutralize the hazard and to help their sagging ego is to downplay those men. They can do this in a condescending or insensitive way as if to demonstrate how little the other person means to them. Or with insults, name-calling, intimidation, and threats, they can go on the defensive to get the other person back into line.

How to Avoid Narcissism?

- **Do Not Fall for Fantasy**

Narcissists can be incredibly charming and irresistible. They are very good at creating a beautiful self-image that attracts us. Their superficial confidence and ambitious dreams draw us—and the more fragile our self-esteem becomes, the more seductive the allure. It's easy to get captured in their network, thinking they are going to satisfy our desire to feel more important, alive. But it's just an imaginary feeling and a costly one.

- **Your Needs Will Stay Unrecognized**

It is worth noting that narcissists are not looking for partners; they are looking for admirers who are obedient to them. The narcissist's primary interest is as someone who can tell them how wonderful they are to help their insatiable ego. It doesn't matter what your thoughts and emotions are.

- **Observe the Way a Narcissist Treats Others**

When the narcissist lies, manipulates, harms, and disrespects others, ultimately, he or she will approach you the same way. Don't fall for the illusion of being unique, and to be spared.

- **Take off Rose Colored Glasses**

It's essential in your life to see the narcissist for who they are and not who you want them to be. Stop making excuses for the wrong behavior, or minimize the harm that causes you. Denial is not going to make that go away. The bitter truth is that narcissists are very resistant to change, so the thing you have to ask yourself is whether you will be able to live like this forever.

• Try Focusing on Your Dreams

Rather than losing yourself in the delusions of the narcissist, concentrate on the things you wish for yourself. What would you like your life to change? What gifts do you want to see developed? What imaginations should you give up to build a fuller reality?

• Keep Healthy Boundaries

Healthy ties are founded on mutual respect and care. But in their relationships, narcissists are incapable of real reciprocity. It's not just because they don't want to; they aren't able. They don't see you. They don't listen. They don't acknowledge you as someone outside of their own needs. Because of this, narcissists regularly breach other people's boundaries. Moreover, they are doing so with an absolute sense of entitlement.

Narcissists think that it's nothing wrong with going through or borrowing your belongings without asking, snooping through your e-mail and personal correspondence, eavesdropping on conversations, barking in without permission, stealing your thoughts, and giving you unpopular opinions and advice. They might even tell you what to think and how to feel. Recognizing these breaches for what they are is crucial so you can start creating better boundaries where your desires are being met.

- **Make a Plan**

If you do have a long-standing habit of allowing others to breach your boundaries, then taking back control is not easy. Set yourself up for success by taking careful consideration of your goals and possible obstacles. What are the most significant changes you are hoping to make? Is there anything you've attempted the narcissist that worked with in the past? Anything it didn't have? What is your balance of power, and how does that affect your plan? How are you going to enforce your borders? Answering these questions will help you assess your options and come up with a realistic plan.

- **Consider a Gentle Approach**

If you need to preserve your friendship with the narcissist, you'll have to tread softly. By pointing out their hurtful or dysfunctional actions, you harm their perfectional self-image. Try delivering the message in a calm, polite, and gentle way. Focus on how their behavior, rather than their motivations and intentions, makes you feel. If they are responding with rage and hostility, try to keep quiet. If needed, go away and revisit the conversation later.

- **If You Are Willing to Keep it, Then Set Boundaries**

To fight against new boundaries, you may count on the narcissist to test your limits, so be prepared. Follow up with any specified consequences. If you send the message back down, you don't need to be treated seriously.

- **Prepare Yourself for Other Changes**

The narcissist would feel upset and frustrated by your attempts to take control of your life. They're used to getting the shots called. To compensate, in other aspects of the relationship, they might step up their demands, short their availability to punish you, or attempt to manipulate or charm you into violating the new boundaries. It is up to you to keep yourself healthy.

- **Do Not Take Things Personally**

Narcissists must always deny their faults, cruelties, and errors to shield themselves from feelings of inferiority and guilt. They will often do so by projecting their own mistakes onto others. It's disconcerting to be blamed for something that isn't your fault or marked by derogatory features you don't have. But try not to take it personally, no matter how difficult it may be. It is not about you, indeed.

- **Do Not Buy into Narcissist Version of Who You are**

In reality, narcissists don't live, and that includes their opinions about other people. Don't let your self-esteem be undermined by their shame and blame game. Refuse to accept unmerited liability, blame, or criticism. That negativity is the one to keep the narcissist.

- **You Don't Need to Argue with a Narcissist**
The instinct, when threatened, is to protect yourself and to prove the narcissist wrong. But no matter how reasonable you are, or how compelling your case, they will not hear you. And

arguing the argument will escalate the situation in a very disagreeable way. Don't run out of breath. Only tell the narcissist that you disagree with their judgment and then move on.

- **Know Yourself**

A strong sense of oneself is the best defense against the narcissist's insults and projections. When you know your strengths and weaknesses, any unfair criticism leveled against you is more comfortable to dismiss.

- **You Don't Need Approval**

It is essential to detach from the opinion of the narcissist. Any desire to please or appease them at your own expense should not be taken. You need to know the truth about yourself, even if the narcissist takes a different view of the situation.

- **Look for Support and Your Purpose Elsewhere**

If you're trying to stay in a relationship with a narcissist, be honest about what you can – and can't – expect with yourself. A narcissist won't change into someone who values you, so you'll need to look for emotional support and personal fulfillment elsewhere.

- **Learn How Healthy Relationships Are Like?**

When you come from a narcissistic family, you might not have a perfect sense of what a healthy relationship is about continuing to give-and-take. You may feel at ease with the narcissistic pattern of dysfunction. Just note that it makes you feel inadequate as usual as it does, too. You would feel respected in a reciprocal relationship, heard to it, and free to be yourself.

- **Spend Some Time with People Giving You Honest Reflection of Who You are**
-

For keeping perspective and avoiding to buy into the lives of the narcissist, it is good to spend time with people who know you and affirm your thoughts and feelings.

- **Make New Friendships Out of Narcissists' Orbit**

Many narcissists detach the people to manipulate them in their lives better. If this is your case, you're going to need to invest time in rebuilding lapsed partnerships or building new ties.

- **Look for purpose and meaning in Work, volunteering, and Hobbies.**

Instead of looking at the narcissist to make you feel good about yourself, undertake meaningful activities that boost your strengths and allow you to participate in your life activities.

- **How to Leave a Narcissist?**

It's never easy to terminate an abusive relationship. Ending one with a narcissist can be particularly tricky because they can be so charming and witty — at least at the beginning of the link or when you're threatening to leave. It's easy to get disoriented by the manipulative behavior of the narcissist, caught up in need to gain their validation, or even feel "gas lighted" and question your judgment. If you are emotionally dependent, your desire to be loyal can outweigh even your need to preserve your self-confidence and sense of self. But an important to remember is that no one in a relationship needs to be harassed, intimidated, or verbally and emotionally violated. There are ways to avoid the narcissist — and the shame and self-blame — and continue the healing process.

- **Get Knowledge about Narcissistic Personality Disorder**

The more you get knowledge, the more you can identify the tactics that a narcissist can use to trap you in the relationship. If you threaten to leave, a narcissist sometimes resurrects flattery and adoration ("love bombing"), which in the first place has caused you to be interested in them. Or they're going to make big promises about changing their behavior that they don't intend to keep.

- **Enlist the Reasons Why Are You Leaving?**

Being straightforward about why the relationship needs to end will help prevent you from being sucked back in. Have your list ready somewhere, such as on your phone, and refer to it when you start having self-doubts or when the narcissist lays on the charm or makes outlandish promises.

- **Seek Support**

The narcissist may have harmed your relationship with friends and family throughout your time together, or reduced your social life. But no matter what your conditions are, you are not alone. Even if you can't reach old friends, you can find help from support groups or helplines and shelters for domestic violence.

- **Do Not Make Threats**

To accept that the narcissist won't change is a better tactic and leave when you're ready. Making threats or declarations will only warn the narcissist and make it harder for you to get away. When you are physically threatened or harassed, seek immediate assistance.

- **After You have Left**

Leaving a narcissist can be a massive blow to their sense of self-importance and entitlement. They still need to nourish their vast ego, so they will often continue to try to exert control over you. If charm and "love bombing" don't work, they can use threats, denigrate you to friends and acquaintances, or stalk you on social media or in person.

- **Cut off All the Connections with Narcissists**

The more you have contact with them, the more confidence you give them that they will be able to reel you back in. Blocking their calls, texts, and emails, and disconnecting from them on social media, is more comfortable. If you have kids together, have someone else with you for every planned parenting handover.

- **It would help if you allowed Yourself to Grieve**

Whatever the circumstances, breakups can be painful. Even the end of a toxic relationship will leave you feeling sad, furious, confused, and crying about the loss of shared dreams and obligations. Healing will take time, so make it easy on yourself and get support from family and friends.

● Do Not Expect the Narcissist to Share Your Grief

Once the idea sinks in that you won't feed their ego anymore, the narcissist would likely move on to manipulate someone else early. We are not going to feel any disappointment or remorse, just that never-ending need for respect and recognition. It is not a comment on you, but rather an example of how their relationships are always very one-sided.

● If You Need Help for Narcissistic Disorder

Many people with NPD are hesitant to admit they have a problem because of the very definition of the disorder— and even more reluctant to seek help. A narcissistic personality disorder may be complicated to manage even when they do. But that does not mean that there is no hope, or that it is impossible to change. For severe cases, mood stabilizers, antidepressants, and antipsychotic drugs are sometimes prescribed, or if the NPD co-occurs with another condition. Psychotherapy is, however, the main form of treatment in most cases. You can learn to accept responsibility for your actions by consulting with a professional therapist, develop a better sense of proportion, and create healthier relationships. You can also work on your Emotional Intelligence (EQ) development. EI is the ability to understand, use, and manage your emotions positively to empathize with others, effectively communicate and build strong relationships.

1.2 Machiavellianism

Machiavellianism is one extreme manipulation type. People with this trait think less about the feelings of others, and more about their ambitions and successes, "relationship therapist Tammy Nelson, explains." Machiavelli wrote The Prince and told a thousand years of killers how to win. "That's why the word" Machiavellian methods "refers to manipulative, duplicitous ways to get whatever you like. And since the other, buzzier elements of the dark triad get all the focus, it seems that Machiavellian characters will fly under the ground, absolutely intact. Plus, the manipulation dimension makes it tough to recognize Machiavellians. I have been wooed many times by opportunistic types who have jumped onto other people to climb to the top. So to help you (well, me) never get confused again with a Machiavellian, I have tried to illustrate the apparent signs that you are in the presence of one.

A Deal Fixation on Power

Ambition is particularly attractive if you can count how many baristas and Musicians you have dated on both hands-what a win, right?! Yet, in all seriousness, though working towards a promotion at work is something to be applauded, it's not so great to get a problem with control — at work, on the dating scene or elsewhere.

A Genuine Cynicism Worldview

The cynicism here isn't an affectionate attitude of believing you've got the worst luck because, of course, the bird's pooping on you again. And it has an overwhelming disdain for the rest of humanity. A Machiavellian is apt to believe that there are losers and that there are winners in life, and that everyone else feels this way, which is not the case.

A Willingness to Exploit Others

One recent study claims that women use dates as free meals flex their Machiavellian muscles. Although it seems like an unjust, sweeping generalization that a gal can't be both romantically interested and very hungry at the same time if she always forgets her wallet? Okay, it is a red flag. Gender, wealth, and favors being wasted on an individual in an arbitrary waypoint to Machiavellianism.

A Self-Centered, Ruthless Desire to Conquer

Anyone who has to talk about their sexual conquests with an emphasis on conquest is someone to avoid When they callously let it be known in their little black book that you are No. 84, that is not honesty. That is very troubling.

A Gas lighting Machine

Gas lighting is a form of manipulation that includes manipulating someone's wellbeing, and if someone you know frequently throws around the term "you're insane," you're probably familiar with the concept. "If you even think your partner has these characteristics, they're a master manipulator, and they're going to stop at nothing to get their way," says Dr. Nelson. "Without remorse, they'll lie, steal without regret, and deceive you into thinking you're the crazy one. As someone asked Dr. Nelson if there were any other visible signs of a

Machiavellian that everyone could watch out for, things got ahem political. I'm going to let you guess what an example she gave.

Alexithymia

Machiavellianism is synonymous with alexithymia, which describes a deficiency in identifying one's feelings and recognizing them. Alexithymic individuals have been characterized as cold and distant and out of touch with their emotional experiences. Alexithymia in Machiavellians is a product of a less understanding of emotions resulting from a shallow knowledge of these emotions, or deficiencies of empathy and mind theory. Whatever the cause, evidence suggests that Machiavellians are individuals who are overly cognitive in their approach to others and themselves, and who are generally out of touch with emotions.

Behavioral Inhibition

According to Grey's theory of reinforcement-sensitivity, the action is regulated by two different neural systems: the system of behavior enhancement, and the method of behavioral inhibition. The behavioral activation system is associated with tendencies to' approach' including extraversion, social behavior, and action. By contrast, the behavioral inhibition mechanism is correlated with traits of' avoidance' such as introversion, steps removed, and' thinking rather than doing.' Recent evidence shows that the behavioral enhancement mechanism associates psychopathy and narcissism with higher levels of activity, while the behavioral avoidance system associates Machiavellianism with more top action. Thus narcissists and psychopaths have more tendency to engage in action-involving and socializing approach behaviors. At the same time, Machiavellians tend to engage more in withdrawn acts and rely on their thinking and intuition. It is consistent with Machiavellians ' image as sly, cynical manipulators conspiring against others, rather than deliberately violating their rights, as would a psychopath.

1.3 Psychopathy

Few psychological terms, like the word psychopath, stir up confusion. Although it is widely used to identify someone with a mental illness, it is not an official diagnosis for a psychopath. To psychology, the true definition of a psychopath is anti-social personality disorder (ASPD), says Dr. Prakash Masand, a psychiatrist and the Centers of Psychiatric Excellence director. ASPD defines a person who demonstrates manipulative and violated behavior to others. Some people may assume that this represents someone who is shy, a loner, who keeps to himself, and so on. That's not the case in ASPD though. When we say 'anti-social' in ASPD, it means someone who goes against society, rules, and other more conventional behaviors.

Common Signs of Psychopathy

As the word psychopath is not an official diagnosis, specialists are referring to the symptoms identified in Anti-Social Personality Disorder.

According to a psychiatrist, some of the more common signs to be aware of include:

- Socially irresponsible conduct
- Disregarding or violating the rights of others

- Lack of ability to differentiate between right and wrong
- Difficulty in showing remorse or empathy
- The propensity to lie frequently
- Deceive and injure others
- Persistent problems with the law
- General disregard for protection and duty someone who exhibits this behavior may also lack deep emotional ties, have a superficial charm about them, be very hostile, and sometimes get very angry.

Those with ASPD also don't care if they hurt others, are impulsive and violent and lack empathy. Abusive doesn't necessarily mean abusive in the case of ASPD.

In addition to the symptoms and habits, Masand states that ASPD is associated with specific traits

- This diagnosis is made by more men than by women.
- Technically you must be 18 years old to receive an ASPD diagnosis. But some people will show symptoms of conduct disorder as early as age 11, which can be an early indicator of ASPD.
- It's a chronic condition seemingly rising with age.
- In humans with ASPD, mortality rates are higher because of their behavior.

Diagnosis of Psychopathy

Since psychopathy isn't an approved mental disorder, the determination by the condition professionals is ASPD. It is essential to mention, before discussing the criteria used to diagnose ASPD, that diagnosing and treating ASPD poses several unique challenges. ASPD can be challenging to treat, according to Masand, a psychiatrist, because the person who needs support doesn't think there's a problem with their behavior. Many rarely seek treatment as a result. As said, the criteria developed for diagnosing ASPD are, that conduct usually starts at age 15 or in adolescence. Masand, however, tells an accurate diagnosis of ASPD is not made until age 18. "The worst of the actions for most people occurs throughout the twenties in the late teen years," he says. A mental health professional will take a full mental health assessment to get a proper diagnosis. The psychiatrist will evaluate a person's thoughts, feelings, behavior patterns, and relationships during this process. You can identify signs and correlate with symptoms of ASPD in the DSM-5. The mental health professional will also look to the history of medicine. The full assessment is a critical step because ASPD tends to show comorbidity with other mental health and addiction disorders. Since an accurate diagnosis of ASPD is typically delayed to the age of 18, adolescents and teenagers with similar symptoms are often assessed as Trusted Source for Conduct Disorder (CD) or Oppositional Defiant Disorder (ODD). CD is more severe than ODD, of the two behavioral disorders. In deciding whether a child has a source of ODD Trusted, clinicians should look at how they behave around people they know. Usually, someone with ODD is more likely to oppose or question family members, teachers, or a provider of health care. If an adolescent or teen shows an ongoing pattern of aggression towards others and regularly makes choices that are contrary to the rules and social norms at home, school, or with peers, a clinician may decide to assess for CD Trusted Source.

Psychopathy Vs. Sociopathy

As with many other psychological terms, psychopaths and sociopaths are often used interchangeably, and it is easy to see why. While sociopath is not an official diagnosis, under the umbrella diagnosis of ASPD, he enters psychopath. There is no clinical distinctiveness between the two. Many people make an artificial distinction based on the severity of the disorder of personality, but that's wrong. That they are trying to say psychopathy is a more severe form of sociopathy, but again, that's wrong. Psychopaths and sociopaths are other words or ways of defining ASPD. The actions seen in both come under the category of ASPD symptoms.

In this chapter we discussed about what is Dark Psychology and what are some basis used in it. The purpose of explaining these was to aware you about the things which can be used for a good purpose and how to avoid things that cause personality disorders as narcissism and psychopathy. In the coming chapters our concern will be unmasking Dark Psychology and letting you know about some new terminologies of Dark Psychology. By reading these you will be in a better way to differentiate between right technique and wrong for controlling mind.

Chapter 2: Unmasking Dark Psychology Terminologies

We hear that knowledge has power. Okay, if knowledge is power, then having human psychology knowledge is the equivalent of having superpowers. Psychology, the concept of the human mind, and how it functions, is a central topic for human existence. Psychology supports everything from advertisements to finance, from a criminal act to religion, and from love to hate. Someone who knows the concepts of psychology holds the key to human influence, a right few others possess. Gaining knowledge of psychology is a challenging task. Like all the most advanced secrets of humanity, psychological knowledge is hidden deep within the pages of dense papers and kept out of reach of the public at large. To order to condense this powerful knowledge into a useful form, someone would need to dig through countless books and papers, trying to separate the valuable from the useless. There's dark psychology in the world at work. You may not like this reality, but you are unable to alter it. So you have a choice: either try to remain unaware of something strong and risk becoming its next victim or take control of your situation and learn to defend yourself and those you love from those who, by their constant psychological manipulation, will destroy you.

2.1 Some Terms Used in Dark Psychology

Undetected Mind Control

"Unnoticed control of the mind is the mortal form of control of the mind in life. If someone is conscious that their mind is being influenced, then psychologically, physically, or socially they can object to it. They will avoid contact or circumstance with the controlling person. A lot of people will run and take over at the first sign of a dangerous person trying to get inside their brain. When their mind controller is undetected, like a jet fighter, then the victim cannot put up their defenses in time. There are two styles of strategies to take over an undetected mind of a person— interpersonal encounters, and media use. Typically, control of the media mind was only possible for large companies, and only interpersonal control of mind was left to individual mind controllers. It is no longer the case nowadays. Laptops and smartphones have explicitly put media mind control powers in the hands of the coldest manipulators who roam the earth.

Hypnosis

Hypnosis is a state of the human conscious mind that requires focused attention and decreased peripheral awareness and enhanced ability to respond to suggestions. The word may also refer to hypnosis-inducing art, skill, or act. Theories about what happens during hypnosis fall into two categories. Other methods describe hypnosis as an altered state of mind or trance, marked by a level of that is different consciousness from the ordinary conscious state. Non-state theories, on the other hand, see hypnosis as a form of imaginative role enactment. A person is said to have increased focus and concentration during hypnosis. The person will focus intensely on a particular thought or memory while suppressing stimulation sources. It is noted that hypnotized subjects have an enhanced reaction to suggestions. Hypnosis is generally induced by a technique known as a hypnotic induction involving a series of preliminary instructions and suggestions. Hypnosis use for therapeutic purposes is called "hypnotherapy," while its use as an entertainment medium for an audience is called "stage hypnosis." Stage hypnosis also happens by mentalists who practice the art form of mentalism.

Deception

Deception is the act of propagating an untrue belief, or not the whole truth (as in half-truths or omissions). Deception may include concealment, propaganda, and sleight of hand, as well as diversion, camouflage, or disguise. There is also self-disappointment, as in bad faith. It can also be named, with various contextual implications: beguilement, deception, hoax, mystification, ruse, or subterfuge. Deception is a significant transgression of relationships which often leads to feelings of betrayal and mistrust between the relationship partners. Deception breaches the laws of association and is seen as a detrimental infringement of expectations.

Most people expect to be truthful most of the time with friends, relational partners, and even strangers. If people see most conversations to be untruthful, it would require distraction and misdirection to acquire reliable information when talking and to communicate with others. There is a significant amount of deceit between some intimate and marital partners. Deception and dishonesty may also provide grounds for tortuous civil action or contract law (where it is referred to as false representation or fraudulent misrepresentation, if intentional), or lead to the conviction of criminal fraud. It also forms a vital part of the denial and manipulation of psychological warfare.

Brainwashing

Brainwashing (also called as mind control, menticide, coercive persuasion, regulation of thought, change of thought, and re-education) is the belief that specific psychological methods and conditioning can modify or influence the human mind. Brainwashing is said to reduce the ability of its subject to think critically or independently to allow the introduction of new, unwelcome thoughts and ideas into the minds of the issue and to alter its attitudes, values, and beliefs. The concept of brainwashing developed in the 1950s to understand how the Chinese government seemed to make people conform to the subject. The concept's advocates also looked at Nazi Germany, some criminal cases in the US, and human traffickers ' actions. Later the idea of mind control was used to justify adherence to certain new religious sects and other communities. It led to a scientific and legal debate, with Philip Zimbardo, Margaret Singer, and some others in the anti-cult movement promoting the concept. At least Eileen Barker, James Richardson, and other scholars, as well as legal experts, rejected the popular understanding of brainwashing.

What is the Motivation Behind Mind Games?

We focused on the inspiration behind manipulative mind games in discussing the distinction between mind games, which are dark and those which are not. The range of motivations that facilitate manipulative psychological games will now be more fully explored. It shows the range of dark motivation that undermines this commonly found Dark psychology manifestation.

One reason that mind games play is to manipulate the victim into performing a specific behavior or thinking, or feeling. In this case, the manipulator may believe their other methods of coercion are not successful and may try something less obvious, like a mind game. The manipulator may also choose to manipulate the target for their sick amusement in this way. It occurs because, as a result of their mental game implementation, the manipulator is seeking to get both gratification and power.

Mind Games

"Mind games are used to describe three forms of competitive human behaviors:

1. One is a mostly conscious search for psychological one-size-fits-all, often employing passive-aggressive behavior deliberately to demoralize or disempower the thinking point. It happens so by making the aggressor look superior, commonly referred to as power games or head games.

2. Unconscious games played by people participating in subsequent transactions they are not fully aware of and which transactional theory considers to be a core element of social life throughout the world.

3. Mental tasks designed to improve mind and personality functioning.

Dark Persuasion

A dictionary may suggest persuading is prevailing over someone to do or believe something using any of a variety of advisory or reasoning methods. There is an aim to distinguish between persuasion and dark persuasion. A persuader may try to persuade someone to do something without thinking about particular strategies or motivation, or without knowing the person, they are trying to persuade. A persuader might be focused on doing the most benefit for the majority of people, such as an ambassador who wants to avoid war between two world powers by establishing political connections where there was none before. A persuader might grasp wildly on straws hoping for something to stick. A dark persuader often perceives the bigger image. He knows who he is trying to convince, what motivates them, and how far to succeed; he needs to take the technique. He's generally unconcerned with his dishonest values. He may see doing the right thing as a perk, but his biggest motivation doesn't have to be. In the morality and self-gratification Venn diagram, the acts of a dark persuader will not always fall into the overlapping field. A dark persuader will see what he or she desires and will devise a way of getting it by any means.

Dark Neuro-Linguistic Programming

One of the critical ideas that tell Dark NLP is that human beings lack any clear identity, and are therefore liable, for better or for worse, to manipulate others. Traditional NLP takes this concept of identity as fluid and uses it to help patients resolve the significant roadblocks that hold them back in life. On the other side, this fluidity of identity means, according to Dark NLP, that an individual can be manipulated into behaving according to others ' will. The people falling under the sway of dark forces like cults or extreme ideologies show this capacity for malevolent influence.

Chapter 3: Common Techniques in Dark Psychology

When we talk about conversions, we are discussing ways we can be more persuasive, more influential. We are interested in meeting and answering the needs of consumers, fans, and followers in a way that appeals to them. So how can you persuade–that is, convert–better? The hacks for conversion and persuasion maybe not surprisingly start with psychology. Knowing why somebody clicks or why they retweet demands that you look at how the individual is wired, the wired way we are all. To understand the power of persuasion and social media, to get to the root of conversion and likes, it helps to know how the audience is thinking and feeling.

3.1 What is Persuasion?

Persuasion occurs when one person forces another to alter. The improvement may be either in their inner mental processes or in their outward behavior. Internal systems contain values, ethics, opinions, goals, and schema. The adjustment may create something new or may extinguish or modify something that already exists.

Elements of Persuasion

- **Intent:** We generally deliberately convince, but we may unintentionally persuade, too. And any interpersonal experience causes both parties to adjust.

- **Coercion:** Coercion wins' obedience where conduct is altered but without any internal involvement or shift in inner mental processes (in reality they can be strengthened in the opposite direction);
- **Context:** The actions modified may be confined to a limited setting.
- **Plurality:** One person or many people can be persuaded; You can even just convince yourself.
- **Presence:** You should communicate with the other person physically (allowing full communication) or by telephone or in writing.
- **Media:** Communication can take place through a variety of media.

While persuasion art and science have been of interest since the Ancient Greeks ' time, there are differences between how persuasion occurs today and how it occurred in the past.

3.2 How Persuasion is Different from the Past?

Richard M. Perloff, in his book The Dynamics of Persuasion: Communication and Attitudes in the 21st Century, discusses the five main ways in which current persuasion varies from past:
The Number of Persuasive Messages Has Increased

For a moment, think about how many advertisements you receive daily. The number of ads the average adult is exposed to every day ranges from 300 to over 3,000 according to different sources.

Persuasive Communication Messages Travel More Rapidly

Tv, radio, and the Web, all help to very, quickly distribute convincing messages.

Persuasion is a Big Business

Besides, the firms that are in business solely for persuasive reasons (such as ad agencies, marketing companies, public affairs firms) and many other firms rely on persuasion to sell goods and services.

Contemporary Persuasion is more Subtle

There are, of course, plenty of advertisements using straightforward persuasion tactics, but many messages are much more discreet. For example, companies sometimes carefully craft a particular image designed to encourage viewers to purchase products or services to achieve that projected lifestyle.

Persuasion is More Complex Now

Consumers are more complex and have more options, so when it comes to selecting their compelling tool and message, marketers must be smarter.

3.3 Types of Persuasion

There are several persuasion concepts or styles. Different types of persuasion have the power to convince people in different ways. If you have someone who is grounded and believes what they can see and hear, then the appeal-to-reason technique will have to be used, while someone who has a little more confidence will respond to the appeal-to-emotion process.

The article will go over all of these methods to help you better understand the different forms of persuasion you can use, and how each person can function on different types of people.

Appeal to Reason

The appeal-to-reason method uses a rational argument, with everything about logic and the scientific method based on persuasion. This method works well with the types of people who need evidence of something and do not support claims that are more based on faith than fact. If you're trying to persuade a group of scientists to follow your belief that the earth revolves around the Moon, then you need a lot of evidence to back it up. Otherwise, you're not going to persuade them into your argument. Just saying it looks like it's revolving around the Moon is an argument that's too faith-centered, and that won't work for the appeal-to-reason approach.

Appeal to Emotion

The appeal to emotion is not based on the evidence but on the emotions a person feels. It can often be a more practical approach for the community as a whole, as people are usually more likely to be controlled by their feelings than their brains. Across history, several examples prove this to be true. With the method of appeal-to-emotion, you will use the faith and imagination of a person to appeal to them and bring them to your argument. Sometimes, you can use seduction, tradition, or even sympathy to get them to agree. Salespeople make excellent use of that process. We cater to your imagination by giving you a picture of a vehicle's test drive so that you can see yourself in the car. You will then sometimes use sympathy to tell you how they might need this deal, as it was a slow month. Some even make use of seduction to appeal. Advertising and propaganda are two further ways to use this form of persuasion. Tradition frequently uses appealing to feelings as a means of getting someone to your side. By using words, "This is the way we've always done it, so we should keep doing it this way," is usually very fine even though there are many other methods available that are more effective than what you're trying to get people to agree with.

There are four aids, with persuasion, that can help convince somebody towards your opinion or idea. Not all of these can be used in written conviction, but the better you comprehend persuasion, the better you are at it, both vocally and through the written word. Such bits of help are:

Body Language

Approximately two-thirds of our communication depends on our body language. For instance, if you want someone to be open to your ideas, you should stand at your side with your hands, palms out like a symbolic gesture of peace. If you're standing with your arms crossed, you're blocking yourself from the receiver, and unconsciously they won't want to deal with you or listen to you.

Communication Skills

The better you speak and write out what you want to say, the more open people are going to be to what you want to say. The person may not be willing to buy because of the poor spelling and wording if you write, "I would like to give you the chance to' bye' my product. But if you say, "I'd like to give you a once-in-a-lifetime opportunity to experience what it means to have free time with this awesome product!" — here on several fronts, you appeal to the guy. Look at various web ads to see how this is done.

Sales Techniques Use Persuasion

This process uses the techniques of established selling; which people can learn over time. Trying only to show good points, appealing to a person's needs, and more, all sales techniques work.

Personality Tests

You can devise a strategy with personality tests that are based on the interaction style of an individual. Many people prefer to talk face-to-face over the phone or e-mail. Some prefer to buy items based on what they see on TV, while others only buy goods when they need it. Understanding how to sell a product or concept to someone originates from the personality of that person.

3.4 Some General Rules When You Persuade

Reciprocity is Compelling

When I do anything for you, you feel obliged to do something for me. Helping each other out to survive as a species is part of our evolutionary DNA. Most specifically, you will systematically exploit reciprocity in your favor. By giving other people little gestures of consideration, you can ask for more back in return, which others will happily provide.

Persistency Always Pays

The person who is ready to keep asking for what they want, and continues to show interest, is the most convincing in the end. Mostly, the reason that so many historical figures have influenced masses of people is by remaining relentless in their actions and message. Consider Abraham Lincoln, who lost his mother, three daughters, a niece, his girlfriend, struggled in business, and lost eight different elections before being elected US President.

Always Complement Sincerely

Compliments affect us all so profoundly, and we're more likely to trust people we feel suitable for. Try to sincerely and often compliment people on things they are not typically commended for, and it's the natural thing you can do to convince others that cost nothing but a moment of thought.

Set Expectations

Much of the persuasion is about managing the expectations of others to trust your judgment. The CEO who promises to increase sales by 20 percent and achieves a 30 percent increase is praised while the same CEO who promises to increase by 40 percent and delivers 35 percent is punished. Persuasion is simply about knowing and overstretching the perceptions of others.

Do Not Assume

Don't ever take for granted what someone needs, always give your value. Via advertising, we should always refrain from selling our goods/services because we feel that many have no money or interest. Don't presume what others can or may not want, offer what you can provide, and leave them with the choice.

Create Scarcity

In addition to the essentials of surviving, virtually all have relative value. We want things because those things are what other people want. When you want anyone to want what you have, you've got to make the item scarce, even when it's yourself.

Create Urgency

You have to be able to instill in people a sense of urgency that they want to act immediately. If we are not motivated enough right now to want something, it is unlikely we will find that motivation in the future. In the present, we have to persuade people, and our most valuable card to play is urgency.

Images Matter

What we see here is more important than what we hear. It may be why pharmaceutical companies are now so open about their medications ' potentially horrible side effects, even set against a backdrop of people enjoying a sunset in Hawaii. Consider your first impressions fine. Then master the ability to paint a picture of a possible experience you can provide for others, in their mind's eye.

Tell the Truth

The best way of persuading someone is to tell them the things that no one else is willing to say for themselves. The most painful, essential things that arise in our lives are to face hard truths. Truth-tell without prejudice or bias, and you will often hear very unexpected responses from others.

Build a Rapport

Everyone likes the real you. It extends to our unconscious behaviors beyond our conscious decisions. By mirroring and matching certain standard practices (the language of the body, tempo, voice patterns, etc.), you can create a sense of connection where people feel more comfortable with you and become more open to suggestions.

Personal Skills

- **Behavioral Flexibility**

It is the person with the most versatility who is in charge, not necessarily the most influence. Kids are often so convincing because they are willing to go through a litany of actions to get what they want (putting, screaming, negotiating, begging, charming) when parents are left with a simple "No" answer. The higher the behavioral arsenal, the more persuasive you will be.

- **Learn How to Transfer Energy**

Many people drain our energy from us while others infuse it on us. The most convincing people know how to move their resources, empower and invigorate them, to others. Sometimes it's as simple as eye contact, physical touch, laughter, or even just active listening in verbal responses.

- **Clear Communication is a Key**

When you cannot describe the definition or point of view to an 8th grader, so that they can explain it to another person with appropriate clarity, it's too complicated. The art of persuasion lies in simplifying it down to its heart, and describing what it means to others.

- **Stay Prepared, and It Will Benefit You**

The point of focus will always be learning something about the people and circumstances around you. Preparation meticulously allows for effective persuasion. For example, in a job interview, you dramatically improve the odds, being fully versed in the products, services, and background of the company.

- **Stay Calm in Conflict and Detach**

No one is more efficient when they're "On Tilt." You'll still have the most influence in conditions of heightened stress by staying calm, focused, and unemotional. In conflict, people turn to those who control their emotions and trust them to guide them in those moments.

- **Use Anger Purposefully**

Conflicts make most people nervous. If you're able to escalate a situation to a higher level of tension and confrontation, certain people will, in many cases, go back down. Use this sparingly, and do not do it from an emotional position or because of a loss of self-control. Yet note, for your benefit, you can use rage intentionally.

- **Stay Confident and Certain about Yourself**

There is no such forceful, intoxicating, and enticing attribute as self-confidence. It is the person who has an unconstrained sense of certitude that can always convince others. When you are sure in what you do, you will still be able to persuade others to do what is best for them, while at the same time getting what you want back.

- **Persuasion is Not Manipulation**

Manipulation is forceful intimidation to get someone to do anything that is not in their interest. Persuasion is the art of convincing people to do things that favor you, too, in their own best interest.

3.5 Manipulation

The method of manipulation is to use indirect methods to regulate behavior, feelings, and relationships. Many people are involved in repeated manipulation, for example, telling someone you feel "good" when you are sad is essentially a form of manipulation because it influences the attitudes and responses of your acquaintance towards you.

Nevertheless, manipulation can also have more-subtle effects and is often related to emotional abuse, particularly in close relationships. Many people view manipulation negatively, mainly when it damages the manipulated person's physical, emotional, or mental health. While people who manage others are doing so because they feel the need to regulate their behavior and climate, an impulse often arising from deep-seated fear or anxiety, it is not healthy behavior. Engaging in coercion will keep the manipulator from communicating with their authentic self, and being manipulated can lead to a wide range of ill effects being encountered.

Mental Health Effects of Manipulation

Manipulation, if unaddressed, will lead to poor mental health results for those controlled. Chronic coercion in close relationships may also be a sign of emotional abuse that can, in some situations, have a similar effect to trauma — especially when the victim is made to feel guilty or embarrassed.
Victims of chronic tampering may:
- Feel anxious
- Develop anxiety
- Develop dysfunctional coping habits
- Always try to please the deceptive person
- Lie about their feelings
- Put the needs of another person before their own
- Have difficulty trusting others.

Manipulation may, in some cases, be so ubiquitous that it leads a victim to doubt their sense of reality. Another such story demonstrated in the classic film Gaslight, in which a woman's husband secretly manipulated her until she no longer trusted her feelings. For instance, the husband clandestinely turned the gaslights down and persuaded his wife that the dimming light was all in her mind.

Mental Health Disorders Because of Manipulation

While most people occasionally participate in coercion, a persistent pattern of manipulation may suggest an underlying concern for mental health.

Manipulation is especially prevalent with the diagnosis of mental disorders such as Borderline Personality Disorder(BPD) and Narcissistic Personality Disorder (NPD). Manipulation can be a way for many with Borderline personality disorder to fulfill their emotional needs or get approval and often occurs when the individual with Borderline personality disorder feels insecure or abandoned. As many people with BPD have witnessed or endured violence, deception may have evolved indirectly as a tool for dealing with the needs.

Individuals with a narcissistic personality (NPD) may have various reasons for manipulative behavior. Since those with NPD may fail to establish close relationships, they may resort to coercion to "win" their partner in the relationship. Features of narcissistic manipulation may include shaming, blaming, playing the "victim," issues of control, and gas lighting. We have discussed these points in the previous chapter in detail.

Manipulation in Relationships

Long-term manipulation, including those involving friends, family members, and romantic partners, can have severe effects in close relationships. Manipulation can deteriorate a relationship's health and lead to the poor mental health of those in the relationship or even relationship breakup. Manipulation may cause one partner in a marriage or relationship to feel bullied, lonely, or worthless. Even in intimate relationships, one partner can manipulate the other unintentionally to avoid conflict or also to try to keep their partner from feeling burdened. Some people may also realize that their relationship is being exploited, and choose to ignore it or downplay it. Manipulation in close relationships can take many forms, including provocation, remorse, gift-giving, or the selective show of affection, deception, and passive aggression. Parents who abuse their kids can set up their kids for shame, depression, anxiety, eating problems, and other mental health problems.

One research also showed that parents who use coercion techniques on their children regularly might also increase the likelihood that their children will use manipulative actions. Signs of coercion in the relationship between parent and child may include making the child feel guilty, a parent's lack of accountability, trying to downplay the successes of a child, and a need to be involved in many aspects of the child's life.

People might also feel manipulated when they're part of a toxic friendship. One individual may use the other in manipulative friendships to meet their own needs at the expense of their friends. A manipulative friend may use guilt or manipulation to gain favors, such as loaning money. They may approach that friend only when they need to fulfill their own emotional needs, and may find excuses when their friend's relationship needs are met.

Examples of Manipulative Behavior

Occasionally, people can unintentionally manipulate others without being fully aware of what they are doing, while others may actively work to improve their manipulation techniques. Some signs of manipulation include

- Passive-aggressive behavior

- Implicit threats
- Dishonesty
- Withholding information
- Isolating a person from loved ones
- Gas lighting
- Verbal abuse
- Use of sex to achieve goals

Since the motives behind manipulation can vary from unconscious to malicious, it is essential to identify the circumstances of the manipulation taking place. Although breaking things off may be crucial in abuse cases, a therapist may help you learn to deal with or tackle other people's manipulative behaviors.

How to Deal with Manipulative People?

If manipulation is unpleasant, it can be challenging to deal with other people's behavior. Workplace manipulation has been shown to reduce efficiency, and loved ones' deceptive actions may make the truth seem questionable.

When you feel exploited in any relationship, it might be beneficial to:

- **Disengagement**

If somebody tries to get you an appropriate emotional response, choose not to give it to them. For example, if you are known to flatter a deceptive friend before asking for an overreaching favor, don't play along — instead, answer politely and move the conversation on.

- **Rest assured**

Manipulation can sometimes include attempts by one person to cause another to doubt their abilities, intuition, or even reality. If this happens, sticking to your story can help; however, if this often happens in a close relationship, it might be time to leave.

- **Tackle the situation**

Please point out the deceptive conduct as it happens. Maintaining an emphasis on how the other person's actions impact you rather than starting with an accusatory comment can also help you settle while stressing that their coercive methods will not work on you.

- **Stay on the subject**

Once you point out a behavior that makes you feel manipulated, the other person can try to minimize the problem, or by ignoring other issues, muddle the situation. Remember, and stay to your principal point.

- **Addressing Manipulation in Therapy**

Treatment and counseling for manipulative behavior can rely in large part on what the behavior causes underlying problems. For example, if an underlying mental health problem triggers the manipulation, individual therapy may help the person understand why their conduct is harmful to themselves and those around them. A psychologist may also be able to help the deceptive individual learn skills to communicate with others while respecting their expectations and resolving underlying insecurities, which may lead to the behavior.

Some mental health disorders, such as borderline personality, may cause people to feel anxious about relationships, leading them to act manipulatively to feel safe. In such situations, a therapist can help the person resolve their mental health issue, which can, in turn, reduce their anxiety and help them feel comfortable in their relationships.

3.6 Persuasion Vs. Manipulation

The principal distinction between persuasion and manipulation is the motive behind the attempt to persuade the other person. Principally, persuasion is done to do good things–promoting the best service and product, making the best match, getting a person to stop doing something harmful. In comparison, manipulation is intended to benefit only one of the parties involved. Persuasion is about the most rational and persuasive way of presenting all of the correct points. Manipulation also implies bending down the truth to achieve the ultimate goal. While persuasion also means talking to a person about doing something they initially did not want to do, it is the honesty and the right intent behind it that makes it socially acceptable. A person may ask a contractor who tried to push a project aside to get it started earlier because they have to move into the house by a specific date. The arguments put forward are real and transparent intention. Manipulating the builder would mean saying the wife is pregnant and is about to give birth at any moment, even though no woman is involved. That is why deception also has a social stigma. It is because people feel they were lied to and coerced into believing something. Another big difference between the two lies in the fact that the person persuaded to take a different view is convinced that this is the best way forward. We have all the arguments given and are armed with whatever they need to make a case in favor of their new option at any time. When it comes to coercion, there's instant remorse after compromise. It is because no real arguments have been used, there is no evidence of good intentions, and the manipulator benefits from all the more.

Chapter 4: Covert Emotional Manipulation

Emotional manipulators use mind games to take power. The ultimate objective is to use the ability to control the other person. A healthy relationship is established on confidence, understanding, and mutual respect. It is true of intimate, as well as professional relationships. Sometimes people try to exploit certain aspects of a relationship so they can profit in some way. There can be visible signs of emotional manipulation. They are often difficult to identify, especially when they do happen to you.

4.1 How are Emotional Manipulation Tactics in Dark Psychology Used These Days?

None of us want to be the target of manipulation, but quite often, it happens. We may not be exposed to someone directly in the Dark Psychology. Still, on a daily basis, we face dark psychology tactics with average, everyday people like you and I. Such strategies are often used in advertisements, web ads, sales techniques, and even the actions of our boss. If you have children (especially teenagers), you will most likely experience these strategies as your kids play with behaviors to get what they want and try autonomy for themselves. The people you trust and love often use covert manipulation and dark persuasion. Here are some of the techniques that ordinary, everyday people use most frequently.

- **Showing Love**

Best wishes, companionship, or buttering someone to make a request.

- **Falsifying**

Untruths, distortion, partial truths, false tales

- **Love Denial**

Holding back on attention and affection

- **Withdrawal**

Avoid people or silent treatment

- **Restriction of Choice**

Giving those choices that separate you from the option that nobody wants to make

- **Reverse Psychology**

Say one thing to a person or do something to inspire them to do the opposite; it is what you want.

- **Semantic Manipulation**

Use terms meant to have a shared or collective sense, but later the manipulator tells you that he or she has a different definition and interpretation of the conversation. Words are important and influential. By knowing these, you will manage to tackle being manipulated. These are to remind us all how easy it is to use those tactics to get what we want. I want to encourage you to assess your strategies in all areas of life, including employment, leadership, romantic relationships, parenting, and friendships. While some people who use dark tactics know with accuracy what they do and are willing to manipulate you to get what they want, others are using dark and immoral strategies without being fully aware of it. Many of these people learned techniques from their parents during their childhood. Others learned the tactics by happenstance in their teenage years or adulthood. They unwittingly used a manipulative tactic, and it succeeded. They did have what they wanted. And they keep using strategies to help them get their way.

People are trained in some situations to use those techniques. Usually, sales or marketing programs are training programs that teach grim, unethical psychological, and persuasion techniques. Most of these programs use dark tactics to make a brand or sell a product only to serve themselves or their business, not the client. Many of these training programs influence people that the use of these tactics is good and is in the buyer's interest. And when they buy the product or service, their lives will be much easier.

- **They Maintain Home Court Advantage**

Whether it's your real home, or just a favorite coffee shop, being in your home turf can be inspiring. If the other individuals often insist on meeting within their domain, they might attempt to create a power imbalance. They claim to own that space, which leaves you at a disadvantage.

For example: "Come when you can to my office. I'm too late to walk to you." "You know how far I'm on a drive. Coming over tonight.'

- **They Come Close Very Soon**

In the typical get-to-know-you process, emotional manipulators could skip a few steps. They "share" their most profound flaws and secrets. Nevertheless, what they are doing is trying to make you feel different so that you can share your secrets. Later on, they can use those sensitivities against you. For instance: "I feel like we just communicate on an intense level. That's never happened before." "I've never had someone like you share their dream with me. We are truly meant to be together in this.

- **They Let You Share Your Secrets First**

With some business relationships, this is a popular tactic, but it can also happen in personal ones. If a person wants to establish control, she should ask questions of sampling so you can share your thoughts and concerns early on. They can then use your answers to influence your choices, with their secret plan in mind.

For instance: "Gosh, I've never heard good things about that firm. What have you been experiencing?" Alright, you're going just to have to tell me why you're crazy about me again."

- **They Twist the Facts**

Emotional manipulators are masters of manipulating reality to confuse you with lies, fibs, or misstatements. They can exaggerate incidents, so they appear more vulnerable. They may also underestimate their role in a dispute to gain support for you. For instance: "I asked a question about the project, and she came to me, screaming how I've never done anything to help her, but you know I do, right?" I cried and didn't sleep a lot all night."

- **They Involve You in Intellectual Bullying**

When you ask a question, someone overwhelms you with numbers, jargon, or evidence, and you may experience emotional manipulation. Some of them presume to be the expert, and their "knowledge" is imposed upon you. That is particularly common in circumstances of financial or sales.

For example: "You are new to this, so I wouldn't expect you to understand." "I know it's a lot of numbers for you, so I'm going to go through it slowly again."

- **They Involve You in Beurucratic Bullying**

Additionally, emotional manipulators in the business setting can try to weigh you down with paperwork, red tape, procedures, or anything that might get in your way. It is a distinct possibility when you express accountability or ask questions that call into question their shortcomings or weaknesses. For example: "This is going to be way too hard for you. I would just quit now and save the effort." "You have no idea what the nightmare you are making for yourself.

- **They Make You Feel Sorry If You Ask Any Question**

When you ask questions or offer some advice, an emotional manipulator may respond aggressively or try to draw you into an argument. This technique lets them manipulate your choices and influence your decisions. They can also use the situation to make you feel guilty in the first place for voicing your concerns. For instance: "I don't understand why you just don't trust me." "You know I'm just an emotional person. I can't help but always want to know where you are.

- **They Always Prefer to Discuss Their Issues**

If you are having a bad day, an emotional manipulator can seize the opportunity to raise their questions.
The goal is to invalidate what you are experiencing. It is, so you are forced to concentrate on manipulators and put your

emotional energy on their issues. For instance: "Do you think this is bad? You do not need to deal with a cube-mate who is chatting all the time on the phone." "Be glad you've got a brother. All my life, I felt lonely."

- **They Act as a Martyr**

Someone who manipulates the emotions of people that enthusiastically want to help with something but then change and drag their feet or look for ways to avoid agreeing to it. They may act like it ends up being a huge burden, and they are going to try to exploit your emotions to get out of it.

For example: "I know this is something you need from me. That's just a lot, and I'm already exhausted." "This is more difficult than it looks. When you told me, I don't think you knew that.'

- **When They Say Something Rude, They Behave as They Were Joking**

Critical comments can be interpreted as sarcasm or irony. They can claim they're saying something in jest when it's planting a seed of doubt that they seek to do.

For instance: "Geez, you look exhausted!" Well, if some of you were to get up and walk around from your office, you wouldn't get out of your breath quickly."

- **They Never Take Responsibility of Their Mistakes**

Emotional manipulators will never be held responsible for their errors. Nonetheless, they will try to find a way to make you feel bad about all this. From the struggle to a failed project. You might end up apologizing, even if they are the ones to blame.

For example: "I just did it because I love you so much." "If you hadn't been to the awards program for your kid, you could have finished the project in the right direction."

- **They Take the Energy Out of the Hall**

Manipulators have a way to go into a room and drag along with them a dark cloud. They want the attention and focus on them, and they want to make sure that everyone in the room notices is upset, unhappy, or unsatisfied in some way. People tend to try to please the manipulator or "feel good" to support them. They may inquire, "Are you OK? Is there anything wrong with that?" It is just the opening to feed the compassion and energy of others that the manipulator needs. A sensitive person will feel exhausted and off-balance when he is in the room with a manipulator.

- **They Always Criticize You**

Without the notion of jest or sarcasm, emotional manipulators may reject or weaken you. Their comments are meant to chip away at your self-esteem. They're supposed to mock you and marginalize you. The manipulator also expressed his weaknesses. For example: "Don't you think that suit is somewhat provocative for a meeting with a client? I suppose that's one way to get the wallet." "Eat is everything you do.

- **They Use Your Feelings Against You**

If you're angry, somebody who manipulates you might try to make you feel guilty about your feelings. They may accuse you of being irrational or of not having invested sufficiently.

For example: "If you loved me so much, you would never doubt me." "I couldn't take that job. I will not wish to be so far from my children. It is the ultimate act of manipulation. The emotional manipulator finds and pokes your fragile Biggest weakness until either you surrender in, or it leaves you feeling like a hound dog. "Without me, you go ahead with the movies. It's all right. I'm going to stay home and finish the laundry. It is always about your needs. If you knew what kind of upbringing I had, you would never ask me to do it. If you are going on the weekend for the kids, go on. I just don't understand how long you will leave the kids. I know we can't afford to purchase a new car. Yet, in my life, I never had a new car. I guess I'll live forever with this crap auto — beautiful things I don't deserve. The emotional manipulating person knows how to play the role of the victim to perfection. They mix up a pot of guilt and sympathy and serve you in ladleful heaping. To get their way, they'll do just about anything— especially if they see a kind-hearted, vulnerable person.

- **They are Passively Aggressive**

Emotional manipulators also attempt to threaten others with aggressive language, overt threats of absolute rage. Especially when they see that you are uncomfortable with conflict, they'll use it to manipulate you quickly and get their way. The goal is to encourage anxiety or intense pain so you'll soon get up on your ass. Each time you bring up her over-spending, your wife may have a temper tantrum. Your husband could raise his voice, slamming doors when you do something he doesn't like. Over time, the manipulator realizes all he or she has to do is get a little mad. They know by this, things are going to go their way.

- **Firstly, They Commit Something, And Then They Forget**

A manipulator can say "yes" to a plan or commit to you, and then when the time arrives to do that, they conveniently forget that they've ever said anything.

Unless you have a video of them pledging, there's nothing you can prove, so it's the "bad memory" against their dishonest phrases. A professional manipulator has a way to twist or replay a previous conversation to suit their needs and make you feel it's your fault, and you're forgetful, greedy, or crazy.

Emotional manipulation causes you to doubt yourself and make you feel bad or guilty that you have called the manipulator into question.

- **In Times of Crisis, They Stay Calm**

Manipulative people often have an opposite reaction to the person they're manipulating. That is especially true in circumstances that are emotionally charged. That's so they're able to use your response to make you feel too vulnerable. Then you measure your reaction based on theirs and conclude that you were out of line. For example: "You've seen everybody else being relaxed. You were just too upset. I do not want to say anything, but you seem out of control a little bit.

4.2 Who Uses Dark Psychology These Days?

- **Narcissists**

Incredibly narcissistic people have an inflated sense-worth (meeting clinical diagnosis). They need others to affirm their belief that they are superior. They've dreamed of being adored and respected. To maintain them, they use tactics of dark psychology, manipulation, and unethical persuasion.

- **Sociopaths**

Genuinely sociopathic people (meeting clinical diagnosis) are often pleasant, talented, and momentous. They use dark tactics to build up a shallow relationship and then take advantage of people because of a lack of emotionality and the ability to feel guilt.

- **Attorneys**

Many attorneys focus so attentively on winning their case that they turn to use techniques of dark manipulation to get the outcome they seek.

- **Politicians**

Many politicians are using dark psychological tactics and tactics of dark persuasion to convince people they're right and get votes.

- **Salesmen**

Many salesmen get so focused on getting a sale that they use dark tactics to motivate and persuade somebody to buy their product.

- **Leaders**

Many leaders are using dark strategies to get obedience from their subordinates. They use these strategies to obtain more considerable effort or higher performance.

- **Public Speakers**

Many speakers use dark strategies to heighten the audience's emotional state of realizing it leads to more products being sold at the back of the room.

- **Selfish People**

It can be someone who has a personal interest ahead of others. First, they will use tactics to meet their desires, even at the detriment of someone else. They don't mind win-losing outcomes.

4.3 How to Tackle People Manipulation?

It can take time to realize that somebody is exploiting you emotionally. The signs are subtle and evolve with time. But if you think this is the way you are being treated, trust your instincts.

- **Seek Apology for Your Part and Move On**

You are probably not going to get an apology, but you also don't have to dwell on it. Own up to what you think you were doing, and then say nothing of the other allegations.

- **You Don't have to Beat Them**

There should be no two people playing this game. Instead, learn to recognize the techniques so that you can practice your responses properly.

- **Know Your Basic Human Rights**

In interacting with a psychologically manipulative individual, the most critical rule is to know your rights and understand when they are violated. You have the right to defending yourself until you harm others. On the other hand, you can forfeit those rights if you hurt others.

There are some of our basic human rights.
- You are entitled to be treated with dignity.
- You have the right to have your thoughts, views, and desires shared.
- You are entitled to set your own goals.
- You are entitled to say "no" without feeling guilty. You are entitled to get what you pay for.
- You have the freedom to have differing opinions than others.
- You have the right to care for yourself and to protect yourself against being physically, mentally, or emotionally threatened.
- You are entitled to build your own healthy and happy life.

Those basic human rights are your boundaries.

The culture is, of course, full of people who do not respect those rights. Psychological manipulators want to strip you of your freedoms, so they can take advantage of you and manipulate you. But you have the moral authority and power to announce it is you who is in charge of your life, not the manipulator.

• Avoid Self-Blame and Personalization

Since the purpose of the manipulator is to try and manipulate your vulnerabilities, it is recognizable that you may feel bad, or even blame yourself for failing to satisfy the manipulator. It is important to remember that you are not the problem in these situations; you have been manipulated to feel bad about yourself so that you are more likely to surrender your power and rights. Consider your manipulator relationship, and ask the following questions:

- Am I being treated with genuine respect?
- Are the expectations and demands of that person reasonable to me?
- Was giving mainly one way or two ways in this relationship?
-

Necessarily, does this relationship make me feel good about myself?
Your answers to those questions give you valuable clues as to whether the relationship's "problem" is with you or with the other person.

• By Probing Questions, You Put Focus on Them

Psychological manipulators will inevitably make demands (or requests) of you. Often these "offers" make you be out of your route to satisfy their needs. When you hear an unreasonable request, it is sometimes useful to put the focus back on the manipulator by asking a few inquiring questions, to see if she or he has enough self-awareness to recognize their scheme's inequity. For instance: "Does that seem fair to you?" Sound fair what you want from me?" Have I got a say in this?" You ask me, or you tell me?" So, what am I going to get out of it?" Do you expect me to [re-establish the unjust request]?"You're putting up a mirror when you ask such questions so that the manipulator can see the true nature of his or her plan. If the manipulator has some sense of self-awareness, he or she will likely withdraw the demand and return. On the other side, genuinely pathological manipulators (such as a narcissist) will ignore your questions and convince them to get their way.

- **A "No" is a Complete Sentence**

Practicing the art of communication is to be able to say "no" diplomatically but firmly. Articulated efficiently, it lets you stand your ground while keeping a relationship. Remember that your basic human rights include the right to emphasize yourself, the right to say "no" without feeling shame, and the right to choose your own happy and healthy life.

- **Take Time for Your Advantage**

In addition to unreasonable demands, the manipulator will also often expect an immediate response from you to enhance their power and influence over you in the situation. During these times, instead of instantly reacting to the manipulator's appeal, consider taking time to your benefit and distancing yourself from its immediate impact. You can exercise control over the situation simply by saying: "I'll talk about it." Remember how powerful those few words are from a buyer to a salesperson, or from a romantic prospect to an enthusiastic pursuer, or from you to a manipulator. Take the time you need to weigh the pros and cons of a situation and decide whether you want to discuss a fairer deal, or whether you're better off by saying' no,' which brings us to our next point.

Confront Bullies

The critical point to remember about bullies is that they choose those they view as weaker, so as long as you stay calm and obedient, you become a target for themselves. But inside a lot of bullies are also cowards. Once their goals start showing backbone and sticking up for their rights, the bully always gets back down. It is true in schoolyards, in households and offices as well.

- **You can Set Boundaries**
  - When a manipulative person becomes aware that they are losing control, their tactics can become more desperate. It is time to make some tough choices.
  - If you don't need to be close to that person, consider cutting them off entirely from your life.
  - If you're living with them or working closely together, you'll need to learn strategies to handle them.
  - Speaking to a therapist or counselor about how to handle the situation might be helpful.
  - You may also be able to recruit a trusted friend or family member to help you identify the activity and impose limits.

- **Set Consequences**

If a psychological manipulator persists on breaching the limits and is not going to take "no" for a response, the outcome will be deployed. One of the essential skills you can use to "stand up" a stubborn person is the ability to identify and demonstrate consequence(s). Expertly formulated, the outcome gives the deceptive person a pause and compels him or her to move from abuse to respect.

Chapter 5: Brain Washing

5.1 What is Brain Washing?

In the early 1950s, Brainwashing was coined by journalist Edward Hunter who wanted to describe the Chinese Communists ' efforts to control the minds and to think processes of the Chinese people after their takeover in 1949. Brainwashing is a method of controlling or influencing the personal beliefs, thoughts, attitudes, or actions of people themselves to make them believe what they had previously considered being false. The word "brainwashing" originated from its Nao, the Chinese term, which means "washing the brain." Brainwashing is a method by which a person or group makes use of strict austerity measures to influence others to the will of the manipulator. But where does he stop honest persuasion and start brainwashing? Today, there are many forms of persuasion employed, especially in politics. For instance, a simple way to persuade a crowd to follow your instructions is first to state a few things that cause a' yes' response, then add items that are actual realities, and finally, recommend what you want them to do.

Methods

- In psychology, the brainwashing study often referred to as the reform of thought, falls into the "social influence" sphere. Every minute of every day, social influence happens. It's the set of ways people can change perceptions, values, and actions of other people. The enforcement approach, for example, attempts to bring about a change in a person's behavior and is not concerned about his ethics or values. It is the strategy of "Just do this."

- Persuasion, on the other side, points for a change of attitude, or "Do it because it will make you feel good/happy/healthy/successful."

- The method of education (which is called the "propaganda method" when you don't believe in what's being taught) goes for the gold of social-influence, attempting to affect a transformation in the person's ideas, along the lines of "Do it because you know it's right."

5.2 Techniques That Are Used in Brain Washing

Isolation

Typically, the first tactic used in brainwashing is to isolate the victim away from his friends and family. The reason for doing this is, so the victim has only the manipulator to talk to, seek their information and thoughts from them. They don't have to worry about any third party coming in and questioning what's happening.

Chanting and Singing

Chanting mantras is an essential feature of many religions, notably Buddhism and Hinduism, and nearly every church has some form of hymn-singing adoration. As each church member chants or sings the same words, their voices merge into one song, creating a strong sense of unity and collective identity. That, along with established singing effects such as lowered heart rate and relaxation, could cast the experience of community worship into a positive light. But the persistent repetition of short intonations in a cult is designed to become mind-numbing, eliminate logical thinking and induce a state of trance. Increased suggestibility is a feature of such a state, and failure to maintain the trance is often followed by the punishment inflicted on cults, ensuring continuous enforcement of ultra-conformist behavior. Psychologists Linda Dubrow-Marshall and Steve Eichel have researched how being exposed to repetitive and sustained hypnotic inductions can affect the ability of the convert to make decisions and interpret new information. They added that continuous lectures, singing, and chanting are used by most cults to alter consciousness.

Love Bombing

Cults want to reinforce the feeling that the outside world is threatening and gravely mistaken. In comparison, they also use "love bombing" to make themselves look accommodating. Love bombing means showering with lavish new or prospective hires and displaying attention and affection. The term has probably originated with either the Children of God or the Church of Unification, but can now be practiced to several different organizations. It is a phenomenon of social psychology that we feel strongly compelled to reciprocate other people's kind acts and kindness. It is, so the counterfeit affection, encouragement, and goodwill shown towards initiates by existing cult members are processed to create a growing sense of debt, obligation, and guilt. Margaret Singer called this an essential character of the cult, useful because it's precisely companionship and validation that many new cult recruits are searching for.

The psychologist Edgar Schein claims that people are triggered into a cult through a process of "unfreezing and refreezing. A new cult member starts to reject his old view of the world during the unfreezing stage and becomes open to the ideas of the cults. The cult solidifies this new perspective during refreezing. Schein mentions to love bombing as a critical point of refreezing — recruits who accept the philosophy of cults are rewarded with hugs and compliments but shunned when they ask too many skeptic questions.

Barratrous Abuse

Most cults hire attorneys to prosecute anyone who criticizes them publicly, no matter how trivial the criticism may be. Of course, the cult can usually afford to lose the lawsuits, while ex-cult members are often insolvent after giving the organization's life. Consequently, many ex-cultists are unable to mount an effective legal counterattack. Moreover, due to the ever-present threat of legal action, mainstream journalists are afraid to criticize cult or reference religious material.

Fatigue and Sleep Deprivation

Our ability to make the right decisions is crumbled by a combination of sensory overload, disorientation, and sleep deprivation. Amway, a multi-level marketing company, has been charged with depriving its distributors of sleep during weekend-long events. It happened because they were including non-stop seminars lasting until the early morning hours, with only brief interludes during which musicians play loud music with lights flashing. A cultivation strategy that is sometimes used in combination with sleep deprivation includes advising participants to adopt special diets that contain low protein levels and other essential nutrients. As a result, the members of the cults will always feel tired, making them powerless to resist the dictates of religious doctrine.

Activity Pedagogy

How does a teacher motivate their students to follow ethical behavior and conformism? The solution is often to integrate some sort of physical exercise or sport into their teaching. Involved in jumping on the spot or running around, and consequently tired, children are less likely to argue or cause trouble. By acknowledging this phenomenon, several cults aimed to have members occupied as a means of control with an endless series of tiring activities. For example, some believe cults such as Dahn Yoga are just physical exercise programs on the surface. Mass sporting events like calisthenics in stadiums in Russia were a recognizable feature of the Soviet system, and historians associate them with the repressive state apparatus. What distinguishes activity pedagogy from mere sports is that the increased mood and group identity experienced after physical activity will be used by a regime or cult to introduce ideological views that could otherwise be met with skepticism. Fatigue by exercise is yet another manner in which the barriers of people can be worn away as a means to enable them to embrace dubious ideas.

5.3 Lifton's Process

Robert Jay Lifton, the psychologist, studied former Korean War prisoners and Chinese war camps in the late 1950s. He determined that they would have undergone a multi-stage process that started with attacks on the sense of self of the prisoner and ended with what appeared to be a change of beliefs. Finally, Lifton defined a set of steps involved in the cases of brainwashing which he studied:

Assault on Identity

You're not who you think you believe you are. It is a deliberate assault on the sense of self of a target (also called its identity or ego) and its core system of beliefs. The agent hides everything that makes the target who he is: "You're not a soldier." "You're not a man." You're not protecting freedom. "For days, weeks, or months, the target is under constant attack to the point of becoming exhausted, confused, and disorientated. His convictions in this state appear less reliable.

Guilt

You are wrong. Whereas the existential crisis is setting in, the agent generates at the same time an intense sense of guilt within the target. He attacks the subject repeatedly and ruthlessly for any "sin" committed, big or small, by the target individual. For everything from the wrongness of his beliefs to the style he eats too slowly, he can criticize the target. The goal starts feeling a general sense of shame, that all he does is wrong.

Self-Betrayal

Please agree with me you're awful. Once the subject becomes disoriented and submerged in shame, the agent pressures him to condemn his family members, friends, and peers who share the same "wrong" belief system that he maintains (either with the threat of physical damage or of continued mental attack). This abuse of his convictions and of those he feels responsible for heightening the guilt and lack of idea.

Breaking Point

Who am I? Where do I stand, and what should I do? With his identity in turmoil, feeling deep shame, and betraying what he has always believed in, the target experiences "nervous breakdown." In psychology, "nervous breakdown" is just a series of severe symptoms that can signify any number of psychological disorders. Wracking sobs, deep depression, and general dizziness may be involved. The target may have lost its grip on reality, and feel completely lost and alone. When the target reaches his breaking point, his sense of self is pretty much up for grabs. He doesn't have a clear understanding of who he is or what's going on. Then, the agent establishes the temptation to convert to another system of beliefs that will save the target from his misery.

Leniency

I can help. The agent gives a small kindness or relief from the violence with the target in a state of crisis. He may offer a drink of water to the target, or take a moment to ask the target what he misses over the home. The small kindness seems enormous in a state of breakdown resulting from an endless psychological attack, and the goal may experience a sense of relief and gratitude entirely out of proportion to the offer as if the agent had saved his life.

Compulsion to Confession

You can help yourself. The target is faced with the comparison between the guilt and pain of identity assault. Then the sudden relief of leniency, for the first time in the brainwashing process, comes. The target may feel a desire to return the favor the kindness that is showed to him, and then, the agent may present the possibility of confession as a means of relieving guilt and suffering.

Challenging of Guilt

It is the reason because you are in pain. After some months of assault, confusion, breakdown, and leniency moments, the guilt of the target has lost all meaning— he's not sure what he's done is illegal, only knows he's wrong. It provides something of a blank slate that allows the agent to fill in the blanks: to whatever he wants, and he can add the remorse, that feeling of "wrongness." The agent attaches the guilt of the target to the creed system, which the agent attempts to replace. The goal comes to believe that the source of his guilt is his belief system. The contrast between old and new has been established:

psychological (and usually physical) agony is associated with the old belief system, and the new belief system is associated with the possibility of escaping that agony.

That's not me; that's my attitude. The battled person is relieved to learn that there's an exogenous shock of his wrongness, that it's not himself who's intractably bad— that means he can escape his wrongness by running away the corrupt system of beliefs. Then he can criticize the people and institutions associated with that system of ideas, and he will no longer be in pain. The goal can free itself from guilt by confessing to actions connected with its old policy of belief. The goal has completed its psychological rejection of its former identity with its full confessions. Now it is up to the agent to offer a new one for the target.

Self -Rebuilding

- **Progress and Harmony**

The agent introduces a new belief system as the path to "good" if you want. At this stage, the agent stops the misuse, providing the target physical comfort and mental calm in combination with the new system of belief. The goal is made to feel it's he who has to choose between old and new, giving the goal the impression that his future is in his own hands. The goal has already abandoned his old belief system in reaction to leniency and abnormality. He is making a "conscious choice" in favor of the opposing belief system helps to mitigate his guilt: if he truly believes, then he has not deceived anyone. The choice is not a hard one: the new identity is safe and desirable because it is nothing like the one that has led to its breakdown.

• Final Confession and Rebirth

I pick good. The target contrasts the agony of the old with the peace of the new. Then the target individual chooses a new identity, clinging to it as a preserver of life. He rejects his old system of beliefs and promises loyalty to the new one that will make his life better. There are frequent rituals or ceremonies at this final stage to induce the converted target into its new community. Some brainwashing victims have described this stage as a sensation of "rebirth."

In a modern laboratory setting, a brainwashing process such as the one discussed above has not been tested because it is damaging to the target and would, therefore, be an unethical scientific experiment. Lifton created this description around the same time from firsthand accounts of the techniques used by the Korean War captors and other instances of brainwashing. Because Lifton and other psychologists have described variations in what seems to be a distinct series of steps leading to a deep state of suggestibility, an interesting question is why some people end up brainwashed, and others don't.

As with brainwashing techniques, the concept of mind control is to remove the old identity and build a new one, a pseudo-personality, one that retains the views, values, and ideas of the manipulators. For example, it tells members of the group that they are in some way, frail and defective. They are members of a culture where society has put on the values and ideas that make them like everyone other. And the community had done this when they were very young before being able to make their own choices. Parents are often blamed for being less than ideal, and members have come to believe the parents were doing them harm.

Thus the members start questioning themselves and who they are.

Psychological trauma is also used in a cult and is caused by sleep deprivation, long working hours, unhealthy diets or heavy-sugar diets, drugs being secretly put into food, and so on. And violence is indeed used in some cults. (Some cult is very vicious, with sexual and physical abuse used to manipulate members. However, members have typically been led to think it's for their good!) Culpability and fear are widely used as part of the general emotional manipulation of cult members. Psychological coercion is also used to make the members feel good about what they do and to discourage any critical thinking. There isn't much thought going on every time we think of potent emotions.

5.4   The   difference   between   Brainwashing Techniques

Cults will also use the following methods to exploit that isn't usually used in the brainwashing techniques mentioned above:
• Hypnotherapy
• The manipulation-double agendas-the target assumes they get one thing, but the truth is they get something else
• Love bombing-showering new members with love and affection to make them feel special.
• Childhood games to induce age regression and promote compliance
• No questioning or criticism of leadership is allowed
• Young participants are usually accompanied by more experienced members and are not given time to think alone

• Cult promotes financial participation as a way of encouraging psychological involvement

• Childhood games to cause age regression and promote obedience • No queries or criticism of leadership is allowed

• New members are usually preceded by more experienced members and are not given time to think alone

• Cult encourages financial engagement as a means of encouraging psychological commitment

Chapter 6: Neuro Linguistic Programming and Dark Psychology

6.1 What is Neuro Linguistic Programing?

- N: neurology–linked to the brain and nervous system
- L: linguistics–usage and impact of the language that we use
- P: programming–activities used to accomplish the expected objectives.

Neuro-linguistic programming (NLP) is a psychological approach involving the analysis and application of strategies used by successful individuals to achieve a specific goal. It applies to different results, feelings, words, and behavior patterns learned through experience. NLP supporters believe that all human actions are optimistic. Therefore, if a plan fails or the bad happens, then the event is neither good nor bad— it provides more useful information.

6.2 A Brief History of Neuro Linguistic Programming

It is generally agreed that NLP began in Santa Cruz, California, in the early 1970s when Richard Bandler, a 20-year-old student of Psychology at U.C. Santa Cruz. It was done when he met and became friends with Dr. John Grinder, who was an associate professor of language studies at the college in his late 20s. Richard Bandler started as a mathematics undergraduate, and also studied computer science. Finally, he became more interested in the world of behavioral science and changed his major. It is often said that NLP started with computer programming and a linguist. Bandler modeled the techniques used in Palo Alto, California by Virginia Satir (1916-1988), American author, social worker, and internationally respected family therapist; co-founder of the Mental Research Institute (MRI). Bandler also modeled the work of Fritz Perls (1893–1970), who invented a method of psychotherapy that he called gestalt therapy. Influenced by the work of Perls, Bandler developed groups of research and gave workshops around gestalt therapy.

Bandler and Grinder joined forces to study the principles that governed gestalt therapy's language structure. They wanted to define the successful therapist's techniques and skills. Whatever worked and removed Bandler and Grinder did not work. They studied Perls and Satir's work, writings, and recordings to extract the essence that made these two therapists extraordinary. How did their work produce excellence? The first two books published on NLP by Bandler and Grinder were Perls and Satir's strategies. The books, published in 1975 and 1976, identified language patterns that are characteristic of competent therapists. Their second book, Frogs into Princes, was published in 1979 as a transcript of an early teaching seminar. After achieving outstanding results, modifying the techniques used by Perls and Satir, Bandler and Grinder started modeling other great communicators. Gregory Bateson had a profound influence on them, and they studied the work of Alfred Korzybski (1879-1950). The studied the work of Milton Erickson (1901–1980), a famous medical hypnotist. These also included the work of Noam Chomsky(1928-present), an American linguist, psychometrician, philosopher, and political analyst who developed transformative grammar near the end of the 1950s.

Bandler and Grinder were fascinated by the methods of Milton Erickson and introduced the conversational hypnosis approach of Erickson into the NLP. In this method, communication is done to the unconscious using "artfully ambiguous" methods and doing away with signs of authority. Erickson focused on building relationships and meeting the individual in their world model to get rid of the inherent resistance. Erickson's methods have become a core part of NLP and are known as the "Milton Model." As expertise and observations generated by Bandler and Grinder, others have begun to extend and contribute to NLP. NLP also includes Leslie Cameron Bandler, Robert Dilts, Judith DeLozier, and David Gordon in their work. Each person contributed to the work done by Bandler and Grinder and helped expand. NLP's passion for and popularity grew out of a collaborative, innovative community of contributors.

NLP keeps on growing through research, sharing ideas, and training. Chris Adlam is Neuro Linguistic Programming Master Practitioner and Frame Persuasion Concepts founder and NLP Business Practitioner.

6.3 What is Done in Neuro-Linguistic Programming?

Dissociation

Have you been in a scenario where you were feeling bad? Perhaps you've experienced something that gets you down every time you think it. Or maybe you're getting nervous in some work situations where you have to speak out in public. Perhaps when you want to meet the "special person" you've had your focus on, you get nervous. While these feelings of shyness, nervousness, or sadness tend to be inevitable or relentless, NLP dissociation strategies can be of immense help.

1. Recognize the emotion (e.g., anxiety, anger, annoyance, a situation dislike) that you wish to get rid of

2. Suppose that you can fly out of your skin and look back at yourself, coming across the whole circumstance from the perspective of an observer

3. Realize the feeling dramatically changes

4. Imagine you can fly out of your body, looking at yourself for an extra boost. This double dissociation would remove almost every minor incident from the negative emotion.

Content Reframing

Use this strategy when you feel pessimistic or powerless in a situation. Reframing can take any negative case and inspire you by having something optimistic about the nature of the experience. Let's assume you end your relationship, for example. That may sound terrible on the surface, but let's reframe it. What are the benefits of being unmarried? You're now open to other possible relationships, for example. You own the right to do whatever you want when you want to. And from this relationship, you have learned valuable lessons that will facilitate you to have better relationships with other people. These are all examples of how a scenario is reframed. You give yourself a different experience of that by reframing the sense of the breakup. It's normal to panic or concentrates on fear in anticipated circumstances, but this only contributes to more complications. By contrast, shifting your focus to the way you have just described helps clear your head and make even-handed rational decisions.

Anchoring Yourself

Anchoring derives from the Russian psychologist Ivan Pavlov who worked with dogs by continually ringing a bell while the dogs fed. Upon numerous bell rings, he found that by ringing the bell at any time, he could see the dogs salivate, even if there was no food in the pot. It created a neural connection called a conditioned response between the bell and the salivation behavior. You can use those kinds of "anchors" stimulus-response yourself! Anchoring yourself helps you associate any desired positive emotional response to a specific phrase or feeling. When choosing a positive emotion or thought, and deliberately connecting it to a small gesture, you can induce this anchor whenever you feel low, and your feelings will change immediately.

1. Recognize what you wish to feel (e.g., trust, happiness, calmness, etc.)

2. Decide where you want this anchor to be on your body, like pulling your ear lobe, touching your knee, or pinching a fingernail. This physical contact will allow the positive feeling to be activated at will. Wherever you pick, it doesn't matter as

long as it's a unique experience you're not doing for anything else.

3. Think of a time when you felt that state in the past (e.g., trust). Go back to that time psychologically and float into your body, look through your own eyes, and relive that moment. Change your body language to suit state and memory. Look at what you've seen; hear what you've listened to, and smile when you recall that memory. You are going to start experiencing the condition. It's similar to sharing a friend with a funny story from the past. As you "enter" the story, you start laughing again, because you are "associating" with the story and "reliving" it.

4. As you return to memory, touch/knock/press the area you've chosen on your body. While you relive the mind, you'll feel the feeling shrivel. The moment the emotional state peaks, release the touch and start wearing off.

5. Doing so will create stimulus-response neurology that will trigger the state when you make that touch again. Just touch yourself again the same way to experience the condition (e.g., Confidence).

6. Think of another memory where you felt the state, go back and imagine it through your own eyes, and anchor the state on the same spot as before, to make the reaction even stronger. The anchor becomes more effective each time you add another memory and will cause a more robust response.

7. Use this strategy whenever you need a change of mood.

Rapport (Getting Other People to Like You)

It is a simple collection of NLP strategies, but they have the power to help almost everyone get along with you. There are many ways to build relationships with other people. NLP comes as one of the fastest and most effective ways. This technique involves a deliberate mirroring of the body language, tone of voice, and phrases of another person. Individuals prefer individuals who are as they are. When unconsciously mirroring the other person, the brain sets off "mirror neurons," receptors of pleasure inside the mind that make people feel like someone imitating them.

The strategy is simple: the other person's sitting down or sitting. Likewise, tilt your head. Smile when they are smiling, Mirror the expression on the forehead. Spread your legs as they navigate theirs — Mirror the tone, etc. Subtlety is the key to creating an unconscious relation. If you're too explicit, the other person might deliberately notice that most likely breaks the relationship. So keep your mirror-smooth and perfect.

Influence and Persuasion

Much of the NLP's research is committed to helping people eradicate negative emotions, restricting attitudes, bad habits, conflict, and more, another aspect of NLP is dedicated to how to manipulate others ethically and convince them.

One mentor in the area, Milton H. Erickson, was a man named. Erickson was a psychiatrist who also researched the subconscious mind using the hypnotherapy (the real, scientific stuff not the dumb hypnosis of entertainment you see in stage shows).

Erickson was so adept at hypnosis, and he developed a way of speaking to other people's subconscious minds without hypnosis. In everyday conversations, he could hypnotize people anytime, anywhere. The Ericksonian form of hypnosis has become known as "Conversational Hypnosis." It's a potent tool that can be used not only to manipulate and convince others but also to help people resolve fears, restrict perceptions, conflict, and more without their consciousness. It is particularly useful when you get across to people who would otherwise be resilient if they know (think young kids who don't want to hear).

6.4   Neuro-Linguistic   Programing   and Communication

Neuro linguistic Programming, or NLP, has become a popular way of talking about human thought and communication for many non-psychologists. It's a version of Popular Psychology. While it's far beyond the reach of our discussion to criticize NLP (because such criticism would cover several issues), you must know a few things about the communication and non-verbal skills and strategies. That is supposed to be efficient and being promoted by both reputable and untrustworthy teachers and so-called master practitioners. Unlike mainstream or popular areas such as linguistics, neuroscience, or psychology, which have their basis in academic research using controlled studies, NLP tends to focus on "what works" and derives many of its methods from other disciplines in practice. So, while several non-verbal communication NLP methods and declarations may have strong research support, it is also likely that some of the techniques and arguments are not validated correctly in controlled study environments.

The message for casual non-verbal communication students is that reading NLP content may introduce you to some excellent and right concepts from fields such as psychology and linguistics. Still, it will also expose you to ideas and assumptions that are not validated or may be invalid. The problem is that you are not going to be able to assess what is valid and what isn't by relying on NLP literature and courses. NLP does not provide a unified theory — it's more of a hodge-podge of useful things.

To make things worse, NLP relies heavily on ads and arguments, unlike more scientific science-based disciplines, and has attracted people who are either inexperienced or dubious for the motives. And who could be called New Age practitioners respectfully?

To explain the range of things that some practitioners include in NLP: the principle or principles are borrowed from linguistics, certainly a valid and agreed way of looking at communication. On the other extreme is the hypnotic regression of past life, which is far outside the limits of accepted scientific practice. Both are deemed part of the NLP. Then, to clarify, marketing claims and professionals who say they can show you how to tell you when people are lying by looking at their eye movements and how to seduce women by applying NLP techniques can be found. It gets messy, and it's hard to separate the NLP's legal aspects from the methods and claims made by NLP charlatans to make a buck (or indeed a lot of dollars) by preying on the ignorance of people.

All this to explain why we don't have nonverbal behavioral elements that are explicitly taken from NLP and not present in more traditional, well-researched, and regulated fields. In this topic, you will find that many things discussed ARE part of NLP, but they are included because they were developed before or outside the NLP community.

The concept found within the NLP is that professional communicators use standard verbal and non-verbal communication techniques to establish interaction with others. Such approaches are based on an understanding of the internal sensory interpretation structures that are used by people to interpret and make sense of their experiences. An in-depth NLP Training will try to ensure that you gain a highly evolved ability to recognize this very subtle form of communication and respond to it. That's because it is one of the necessary skills that much of the' magic' of NLP depends upon. Applying NLP to communicate expertly, or to develop excellent relations, or coaching someone in personal development or using most of the well-known NLP techniques requires you to have a unique ability to recognize nonverbal communication.

How to Do?

1. Choose one area and stay with it for a week or two then move on to another. Just do your "Voice Tonality Time" for the next few weeks. Use this time to hear the tones of the voice real. (This is a high starting point since you can do it on the phone as well.)

2. In any conversation for the first 90 seconds (only), pay the most attention to the tonality of the other person's voice. Forget about it after 90 seconds, and carry on as usual.

3. Summarize what you've learned and remembered at the end of the day. Do this by talking or writing about your observations in a diary-or both. It is developing the ability to sharpen your sensations-or Sensory Acuity, in NLP jargon.

4. When you get better at hearing subtle changes in tonality, you also begin to guess or ask the person that what has transformed their mood, if appropriate. It is the development of calibration skills–learning to recognize what a specific shift signals about the person you're talking to.

That is all you have to do. After doing this for a few weeks, your Sensory Acuity and Calibrate ability in this area will have significantly improved. Now switch to another area. You could start studying the relationship between, say, breathing patterns, and shifts in mood.

Words of Caution

It's not an excellent way to show off your newly developed skill as a kind of party piece or a trick about "I can read your mind." People are quite sensitive about how you react to their nonverbal communication. Displaying a lack of respect for it may well create animosity in the long term. Conversely, recognizing and responding to non-verbal communication with respect and appropriateness is one of the most effective ways of developing and maintaining relationships. Providing you attract a person's conscious attention to what you're doing or what you've accomplished, your skill in this field can improve your ability to build and sustain consistent, intimate, social, and professional connections.

6.5 Hypnotism

When most people read the word "hypnotism," they think of a guy with a mustache and a top hat waving a pocket watch while asserting that someone "goes very sleepy." Believing in this generalization is, in fact, hazardous. It is because there are actual hypnotists who are equipped with subtle but effective techniques. These people can draw upon the darkest psychological elements to influence people in an incredibly powerful way. So if hypnotism isn't a stage hypnotist's old stereotypical image, what exactly is hypnosis? In simple words, it's the ability to make suggestions to someone flowing through deep layers of their consciousness. This ability to make profound, impactful suggestions to someone while in a fragile and suggestible state gives a high degree of power to hypnotic dark manipulators over their victims. Like almost any other technique in this book, hypnotism isn't something people encounter in their daily lives in a milder, more reliable way. Hypnotism can take the form of suggestive practices, which are both verbal and nonverbal. The recommendation types are often very subtle, and therefore hard to detect. Hypnosis works, by its very nature, at the deepest levels of a person's mind. Someone capable of generating a hypnotic state and reaction in someone will be able to bypass their defenses and manipulate them without raising alarms or allowing a person to build their guard.

Hypnotic Tactics

As you have developed the concept between what hypnosis is a generalization and what it is, it's time to explore the main hypnotic tactics. These types of tactics have many variations, but they offer an insight into the main things to be careful of.

Suggestion Therapy

If hypnotism can be understood as "strong suggestion" in a darkly psychological sense of the word, then it is essential to understand what exactly is meant by suggestion here. Some people would think that an idea is a clearly stated assertion, like "I suggest you do this." The dark view of suggestion in psychology is very distant from the common understanding of the word. The first important concept to understand is the fact that it can be either verbal or nonverbal hypnotic suggestion. Picture an iceberg on the human brain. The part of the iceberg on the water surface shows the established and understood facets of cognitive function, such as thought. The broader, more in-depth section of the ice frozen beneath the water covers actively inaccessible and little known parts of the brain. Should you doubt the capacity of this secret portion of the brain, you need only think about dreaming and the immense power of the mind to produce a series of images, objects, and sounds while a person is asleep. Dark hypnotists work toward this secret, subconscious part of the brain.

There are two forms of suggestion commonly used by hypnotists— quiet and verbal. Both types of hypnotic techniques come in diverse ways. A range of factors depends on the exact kind of hypnotism a deceptive person chooses to use at any given time. Some manipulators will execute whatever form of hypnotism they feel is most impacting on the particular psyche of their victim. Others perform whatever technique they may wish to use at the time for their amusement. It largely depends on whether the hypnotist seeks to exert influence in the most compelling manner possible, or is merely trying to control someone for their fun and games.

Verbal feedback can be tough to detect. At times, dark hypnotists will inject thoughts into the minds of their target using words that sound identical to other, more innocent words. To take a very dark example, if a hypnotist wanted to instill suicidal feelings into their audience, they could disguise the actual command of "You want to die" as something similar sounding like "You want to dine." The hypnotist would speak the words "you want to die," but in a way that would mask the real content. For example, the hypnotist could talk about an upcoming trip and say, "You have to check out the local restaurants, you want to die, somewhere that's popular but picturesque." The mind of the victim would absorb the suggestion of death without knowing why!

The example above of masked verbal suggestions resembles a poison that is hidden in somebody's food. The victim absorbs the hidden content, believing they appreciate something positive and harmless when they ingest something mortal. The particularly devastating part of this strategy is the fact that the victim never will notice it. Even if someone thought he'd picked up on the hypnotist's actual words, imagine how crazy they'd sound calling them out! People will generally take whatever option is psychologically more natural for them, and will, therefore, accept without question the masked command.

Verbal (Communication) Suggestions in Hypnosis

One form of verbal persuasion is the tone of voice and word choice of a hypnotizer. Many hypnotists will be deliberately studying the speed and delivery style that a specific client uses when they convey something dramatic. For example, if someone wants to say something important, their voice lowers in pitch and slows in speed, the information would be memorized by the hypnotist and stored for future use. In that exact, mirrored tone of voice, the hypnotist would then make suggestions to the victim.

Thanks to the carefully modulated tone, the words expressed in that vocal variation would penetrate deeply into the defenses of a victim. Because the hypnotist would only express the provocative material in that tone of voice, and then switch back to their usual way of speaking, the victim would not even be aware of what had occurred. Another form of personalized, verbal suggestion that a hypnotic user of dark psychology employs is to pick up words that have a unique, intense meaning for the victim that uses them. For instance, when someone is emotional, they will often use a specific term to describe the feeling. If the hypnotic manipulator can pick up on these personal words, then they can deploy them to their advantage. Just as people have a particular tone of voice, they have a list of own sense words, without understanding it very often.

The manipulator will get a better understanding of their target than the victim does. Knowing these words and tones, the manipulator can use the victim's brain in reverse engineering against them.

Non-Verbal Suggestions During Hypnosis

Even suggestions can take nonverbal forms. It can be through the body language of the hypnotic manipulator, or even the signs they place in their surroundings. If you do not think these seemingly trivial things might exert a hypnotic effect, then think again! Even political leaders used such strategies in ways like altering their hairstyle to express a particular purpose during speeches. As discomforting as it is to believe, the human mind is profoundly susceptible to even the slightest hints and indications.

And what are some of the main ways that a hypnotic manipulator can use against his victim through nonverbal suggestions? The methodology revolves around the partnership concept. A skilled hypnotist can consistently associate a strong emotion with some kind of external stimuli, such as a particular movement of the eyes they use. For example, if a hypnotist wanted to be able to cause a feeling of panic in a person, they might choose to make a particular movement of their eyes whenever the victim thought about, or felt, panic. The subconscious of the victim would then learn to associate the evolution of the eye with the sensation. The hypnotist will, over time, be able to trigger the emotional response by merely making the eye movement, even without any other stimuli required. An environmental stimulus is another form of nonverbal suggestion which is a part of the toolkit of the hypnotist. Think of environmental stimulus as being summoned like a child to the office of the principal. The place itself was enough to send you into a deep panic feeling as you had learned to connect the location with fear and issues. Hypnotists can use this same concept in adult life to devastating effect.

For instance, they'll often be sure to have a specific type of discussion with a victim only in one location. Picture a hypnotist in a romantic relationship with their victim. Every time the hypnotist wants his victim to get some kind of agreement or consent, he may be sure to ask her only when they're in a particular coffee shop. Over some time, the mind of the victim begins to associate the coffee shop's physical environment with the permission being granted. The physical environment can then be used as an external psychological weapon by the hypnotist if he has to exert influence and control. I have discussed about the dark persuasion, hypnosis, manipulation, brainwashing and other mind controlling techniques. In this chapter I also told you about the Neuro linguistic technique and how it can help in tackling a situation. But in the last chapter I will tell you about emotional intelligence and how it will help to rule your mind as well other. You will also come across the tips to improve your emotional intelligence as it is basis for making a powerful decision.

6.6 Deception and Tactics

Deception is a hallmark of dark psychology. Like many other dark psychological tactics, it can be hard to tell if any given instance of deception is ambiguous or not. Lying and deceit are the same things that would be claimed by many people. That is wrong. Lying is a form of deception but is by no means the only kind of deception that can take place. Instead of thinking of deception as "lying," it is better to think of it as "misleading." Any action or word capable of making someone believe anything other than the truth can be accurately called deception. So what are some frequent disappointments? Lying, omitting the facts, suggesting lies, or fraudulently proving something incorrect are all forms of deceit. You'll probably realize at some point that you've done some of those things yourself. Does that suggest that dishonest behaviors are manifestations of dark psychology? Neither at all.

To some extent, everyone deceives something or something else. People can mislead others for a range of reasons, such as honesty, humiliation, or inadequacy. Studies have shown, for instance, that many, even most men on dating websites, will lie about their height. It doesn't make them Dark Psychology professionals! People are even deluded by a range of issues, including their health, ambition, and happiness. Such regular, daily examples of deception are not tantamount to dark deception. So what is it that does?

Deception can be seen as obscure when it is performed with either contrary or indifferent intention towards the deceived person. Usually, normal deceit is driven by an inability to face the facts in one way or another. On the other hand, dark deception is an awareness that the truth does not support the deceiver's deceiving aims. Thus, the truth is either altered, hidden, or ignored for favoring of events that better suits the purpose of the deceiving person. Put, people who use dark psychology use trickery to hurt, not help. They are promoting their interests but at any cost, no matter who gets hurt.

Deception Tactics

So you understand precisely what dark deception is about, its scope, and the common areas where people are fooled. Now it's time to carefully examine the specific tactics manipulators use to deceive darkly. Each of the tactics is equally powerful, and at its most impactful and harmful time, careful manipulators know precisely how to use each. It's important to note that manipulators won't alternate neatly between the following four categories— any deception will likely involve a mix of each. Lying is perhaps the most prominent and popular type of dark trickery. When the manipulator has determined that their target is vulnerable to deception and unable to gage the facts, they choose it as a technic. It may be because the victim is a relatively trusting person, or the manipulator has worked carefully over time to lower their guard on their target. If a manipulator has chosen to deceive by using lies, then it is likely that they have also considered a way to hide their lies and explain any discrepancies that the victim might notice. Manipulators are masters of getting a "plan b" in their dark deceptions at any given time. Lying deceit is likely to occur in a subtle and thought-out way. Over time, a skilled deceiver will likely embed their lie into truthful information. For example, a manipulator is likely to tell a story that is true at 90 percent and false at 10 percent. The victim will perceive the story as entirely accurate and has no way to separate and determine the truth about the 10 percent deceptive. Many manipulators spend time associating reality with a familiar tone of voice or gesture, too. Then in this tone of voice, or with this expression, they will say something falsely misleading, and it is likely to be perceived as real by the subconscious of their victims. Implying is a subtler form of trickery than lying out and out. Implication involves suggesting that something is right rather than boldly stating that it is. Let's take one example to illustrate this notion. If somebody were to trick a victim about how much money they've got, then they could either lie or say. A lie would sound like, "Oh, I'm a good guy. I made a lot of money,' while the manipulator knows that's not the case. An implication may take the form of a "trying to handle things with my accountant is so stressful.

My lot of time is used in trying to get my tax bill down. "The manipulator behaved and spoke in a way that implies that they are rich without saying it flatly.

Chapter 7: Emotional Intelligence

We probably all know people who are excellent listeners, either at work or in our personal lives. They always know what to say–and how to say it –so that we are not annoyed or upset, no matter what kind of situation we are in. They are concerned and respectful, and we usually leave them feeling more confident and positive even if we don't find a solution to our problem. We know people who are masters in managing their emotions, too. In stressful situations, they do not become angry. Then, they can look at a problem and find a solution calmly. They are excellent decision-makers, and they know their intuition when to trust. Nonetheless, regardless of their abilities, they are usually willing to take an honest look at themselves. They make good criticism and know when to use it to improve performance. People like this have a high level of intelligence on the emotion. They know themselves very well, and they can also sense other people's emotional needs. Now more people accept that emotional intelligence is just as critical to professional success as technical ability; it is increasingly used by companies when recruiting and promoting. One significant cosmetics company, for example, recently revised its hiring process for salespeople to select candidates based on their emotional intelligence. The Outcome? By average, people hired with the new system have earned more than salespeople picked under the old system. Employee turnover among the group selected for their emotional intelligence has also been substantially less. So, let's know what is emotional intelligence, correctly, and what can you do to improve yours?

7.1 What is Emotional Intelligence?

Emotional intelligence refers to the ability to identify and manage one's own emotions, as well as other's feelings. Psychologists Mayer and Salovey (1990) coined the term ' Emotional Intelligence ' for the first time. Goleman (1995) identified five distinct categories of skills that are the critical features of EI and proposed that, unlike the intelligence quotient (IQ), these specific skills can be acquired where they are missing and strengthened where they are present. Thus, emotional intelligence, unlike its relatively fixed cousin, IQ, is instead a dynamic aspect of one's psyche and includes behavioral traits that can yield significant benefits when worked on, ranging from personal happiness and well-being to elevated professional success.

7.2 Categories of Emotional Intelligence
Self-awareness

The ability to understand and accept one's feelings and their effect on others. Self-awareness is the first step towards contemplative self-assessment. It helps one to recognize the behavioral and emotional aspects of our psychological makeup that we can then aim for improvement. Psychological self-awareness often includes understanding what motivates you and, in effect, what brings fulfillment to you.

Self-regulation

The ability to manage one's own harmful or destructive feelings and respond to situation changes. People skilled in self-regulation excel in conflict management are well adapted to change and are more likely to assume responsibility.

Motivation

It is the desire to motivate oneself, with an emphasis on gaining internal or self-gratification as opposed to external recognition or incentives. Individuals who can inspire themselves in this way have a propensity to be more involved and centered on the goal.

Empathy

The ability to understand and accept how others feel and acknowledge certain emotions before reacting to social situations. Empathy also helps an individual to consider the factors shaping relationships, both personal and on the job.

Social Skills

The ability to manage other people's emotions by emotional understanding and using this to build relationships and connecting with people through skills such as verbal, nonverbal communication, and active listening.

7.3 Importance of Emotional Intelligence

In terms of personal and professional success, the significance and advantages of emotional intelligence are enormous. In many vocations, it is a core competency, can support advancement to studies and professional achievements, improve relationships, and enhance communication skills; likewise, the list continues. Bar-On (1997) continues so far as to recommend that people with higher emotional intelligence tend to perform better in life overall, regardless of IQ, than those with lower EI. There has been much discussion about the benefits of teaching EI in schools, with an emphasis on the idea that emotionally smart kids grow up to become emotionally intelligent adults.

Physical Well-being

The capacity to take care of our bodies and, in particular, to control our tension, has a high effect on our overall health, is strongly tied to our emotional intelligence. We can only expect to manage stress and maintain good health by being aware of our emotional state and our responses to stress in our lives.

Mental Health

Emotional intelligence influences our approach and attitude to life. It can also help relieve anxiety and avoid mood swings and depression. A high level of emotional intelligence corresponds with a positive attitude and a healthier outlook on life.

Relationships

We become better able to communicate our thoughts more constructively, by better understanding and controlling our emotions. We're all better able to understand and communicate with those we're in relationships with. Knowing the needs, feelings, and reactions of those we care about leads to stronger relationships that are more fulfilling.

Better Conflict Resolution

When we can determine the emotions of people and commiserate with their perspective, it is much easier before they start to resolve conflicts or possibly avoid them. We're all the better at persuasion because of the very essence of our ability to understand others ' needs and desires. When we can understand what it is, it's easier to give people what they want.

Success

Higher emotional intelligence helps us become better internal motivators, which can minimize procrastination, improve self-confidence, and strengthen our ability to focus on a goal. It also helps us to create better support networks, to tackle challenges, and to persevere with a more robust outlook — the ability to delay gratification and see the long-term impacts the ability to be useful.

Leadership

The ability to understand what motivates people, to respond positively, and to build stronger working-place relationships with others inevitably makes those with higher emotional intelligence better leaders. An effective leader can recognize what his people's needs are so that those needs can be met in a way that promotes higher performance and satisfaction in the workplace. An emotionally savvy and intelligent leader can also build stronger teams by making strategic use of their team members ' emotional diversity to benefit the group as a whole. Emotional intelligence is not yet fully realized, but we know that in the overall quality of our personal and professional lives, emotions play a vital role, even more, crucial than our actual brain intelligence assessment. Technology and equipment can help us learn and master knowledge; nothing can replace our ability to learn, control, and master our emotions and those around us.

7.4   How to Develop Emotional Intelligence?

Observing Your Feelings

When we are too busy worrying about what to do next, and what can be done better, we quickly lose touch with our emotions. Instead of taking good care of our feelings, we most often choose to ignore them. What we do not know is that suppressing our feelings exacerbates issues. The more we try to back down our beliefs, the more uncontrollable our emotions are. If we have an emotional reaction to something, it may be because we have some unresolved problems. So when you feel like having a few negative emotions next time, calm down, and think about why you're experiencing this. Breathe deeply and write down your feelings and possible reasons.

Try to Respond not to React

Reacting is a subconscious process in which we act in an unconscious manner that expresses or soothes an emotion. Responding is a conscious process involving paying attention to your sensations and deciding how to work.

When you are more conscious of your emotional triggers, you can always think ahead of time about the way you will behave.

For example, if you know that when you feel tense at work, you get angry quickly and throw anger to colleagues, take note of that and think about what you can do next time you experience the same stimulus. Maybe you can try to tell your boss that you need some moments of silence because you're feeling anxious right now, or perhaps you can have a few minutes of alone time to calm down first.

Stay Humble to Others

If you always think you're better than others, you're not going to see your faults, and you're probably going to get emotional about things that don't meet your expectations. Try to look from a different perspective at the same thing. Instead of criticizing someone or something, put yourself in the shoes of someone else and try to think or behave like them: would you do the same thing or feel the same way too, and why? In this way, you are likely to understand the thoughts and emotions of other people more; and in similar situations, you will also learn something new about how to deal with things too. Be humble enough to know that you are no better than anyone else and wise enough to know you are different from the rest!

Chapter 8: Case Studies from History

8.1 Case Studies

You now know the main concepts behind dark psychology and how, in a variety of situations, these theories are applied. It is powerful, but not enough on its own. You'll see the arguments brought to life in this book by taking the time to learn about dark psychology through the study of real-world case studies. The case studies are eye-opening, fascinating tales in their own right. We give an insight into some of this planet's most mentally unusual types of people ever made. To a budding disciple of dark psychology, each case study is laid out in a way that is as useful as possible.

Factual information surrounding each case study is given before extracting and simplifying psychological insight. Each case study will then be linked directly back to the dark psychology found in this book to enable you to understand it in a more meaningful and richer way. The instances in this chapter are the most extreme examples of dark psychology in all of human history. We are given not to be glorified, or even punished, but instead gained from it.

The Modern Machiavelli-Hitler

There are many comparisons to find between Machiavelli's political ideas, as conveyed by "The Prince," and Adolf Hitler's political career. Therefore, the point could be made that Hitler is the best possible example of what looks like a real, modern Machiavellian dictator. Next, we will have a look at the parallels between the thoughts and actions of Hitler and those of Machiavelli, before discussing the insights into Machiavellianism as a quality that Hitler provides. One of the first parallels that can be made between Machiavelli and Hitler is the statement in "The Prince," that in a never-ending war, peace should only be seen as a brief respite. Hitler was committed to destroying and eventually planning to take over the whole world under his authoritarian Third Reich. Hitler is, therefore, the closest thing to Machiavelli's idea of an unceasing warrior ruler that the modern world has ever seen.

Machiavelli has also been a proponent of creating and manipulating reality to sort out a predetermined political objective.

The persecution and subsequent extermination of the Jewish population of Germany were infamously one of Hitler's core doctrines. The false flag operation, known as the Reichstag Fire, was one of the critical events that helped Hitler achieve his genocidal target.

Whether Hitler engineered this event to suit his anti-Jewish and anti-Communist schedule is a matter of debate. Still, a large number of evidence suggests that he did precisely that. Regardless of the exact circumstances, the incident is a powerful example of the use of a Machiavellian false flag technique to achieve an entirely different purpose. One of the key ideas behind the political thinking of Machiavelli, and subsequent Machiavellian individuals, is that power is in and of itself a worthy end goal. They are justified according to Machiavelli's blueprint of how a leader should behave, no matter what methods are used to hold on to and retain power.

Hitler is an example of that principle in practice in a textbook. Hitler knew how the political system of the time and the hearts and minds of the German people could be manipulated. There is a strong suggestion that Hitler might have escaped Nazi Germany and fled to live the rest of his days surrounded by fellow Nazi escapees in Argentina. But this is a possible example of never letting go of power, even in the face of apparent death.

Perhaps the most critical and undeniable connection between Hitler and Machiavelli is the idea of "it's easier to be respected and hated, but if that's not possible, fearful rather than loved." It's easy to overlook the kind of loyalty, affection, and even worship that Hitler was able to inspire in the German people of the period. History since World War Two has painted Hitler as the epitome and embodiment of the evil, the closest thing ever seen by the Earth to Satan's incarnation. Nevertheless, at the time, Hitler was equally adept at inducing love and fear responses. One only has to watch a video of Hitler's speeches to see that Hitler was able to evoke the combination of awe and fear.

Insights and Links with the Dark Psychology

One of the main Machiavellian concepts to emerge from "The Prince" is the idea of failing to keep your word, your pledge, unless it is in your interest to do so. Machiavelli stresses the need to appear honest, at least, no matter what the reality of the situation may be. Hitler provides a real insight into how real-world political power figures are capable of implementing this concept. One trademark feature of Hitler's discourses was that they delivered epic and hard-to-implement promises that would never come to fruition realistically. Even though Hitler could not read on the ideas he put forward in his rhetoric, he managed to maintain the image of being a man striving to deliver on his word. It is a clear example of the Machiavellian philosophy of distinguishing reality and public perception from a powerful psychological influence in the real world. Another Machiavellian principle exemplified by Hitler was power-building and threaten-elimination. Hitler systematically eliminated anyone who opposed his quest to lead Germany back to its former glory.

He ultimately killed anyone who stood in his way — former allies, competing for ideology holders or ethnic groups Hitler felt the need to rid Germany of it. This consolidation of power has allowed Hitler to exert as much influence as he has. It shows that, in practice, even in the modern era, the Machiavellian theory is indeed valid. Hitler's final insight into the world of dark psychology is his use of, and enthusiasm for, sadism. This Dark Tetrad quarter is especially evident in the way in which Hitler treated those forced into his concentration camps. These poor souls ' fates included torture, medical experiments, and death by starvation or gassing.

A study from History's Narcissistic Dictators

One of the narcissists ' classic characteristics is their perception of status and self-worth to far beyond anything that is supported by fact. This usually leads people with an inflated ego to be trapped in lifestyles and situations they see as being fundamentally underneath. Sometimes someone with a narcissistic personality is born into a situation in which they have the power and the status to express their narcissism fully. Nothing more exemplifies this than some dictators of history who possessed the power and control to match their egos. Here are some of their tales.

Saparmurat Niyazov is one of the best examples of a narcissist being able to satisfy grandiose inclinations. He took over as Turkmenistan's leader and was able to tap into a power vacuum left by the collapse of Soviet ideology. His ascension from leader to the pure manifestation of narcissism began when he decided to be Turkmenistan's president for life. From there, some memorably, selfish choices led to total power. One of the more infamous aspects of Niyazov's rule was that the months of the year had been renamed to reflect his glory. In keeping with his whims, he has introduced bizarrely specific laws, such as limiting the presence of people and renaming common everyday items according to what he thought they should be named. Perhaps the most potent illustration of Niyazov's grandiosity was his creation of a religious text that gave equal status to existing scriptures such as The Holy Qur'an within the nation. Other dictators have produced similarly "revered" documents, such as Colonel Gaddafi of Libya. It is a known trait perhaps best demonstrated by the status afforded within Nazi Germany to Adolf Hitler's "Mein Kampf."

A more known, yet equally terrifying, dictatorial dynasty is that of North Korea's leaders.

Current dictator Kim Jong Un and his father Kim Jong Il are endowed with the status of deities within their tightly controlled nation, and this is reflected in the "facts" that North Korean citizens have about their life. For example, at his first attempt at the sport, Kim Jong Il is remembered for shooting a golf round, which consists of all "holes in one." Citizens of North Korea are so tightly indoctrinated into the cult of political personality that governs their lives that they often take such claims face value.

Insights and Links to Dark Psychology

So what can narcissism teach us about such outlandish examples? Many of the traits that such dictators display are examples of how controlling and pedantic narcissists become when they are given enough power to fulfill their wishes. Let's take one example of North Korea. It's claimed that the new leader, Kim Jong Un, had his uncle killed in a meeting for yawning. The execution method? An anti-aircraft weapon which can destroy the fighter jets. It is an example of the need for flattery and anger on the part of the narcissist when not receiving it brought it to its logical conclusion. The many instances of rulers who create theological, moral, or philosophical treatises that are then elevated to the level of necessary, sanctified reading within the country is an example of the narcissistic idea of being "special" and "equal to the greatest figures of mankind." In the minds of narcissists, they are the contemporaries of prophets and saints, a scarce species.

If you can understand the degree to which they genuinely believe this is the case, then their publishing of such egotistical texts begins to make some twisted sense.

Conclusion - Part 1

People understanding psychological tactics are holding the key that others can't have. Dark psychology is a topic of discussion around the world, and different people are using it for various purposes. It contains three primary components that are narcissism, Machiavellianism, and psychopathy. The individuals belonging to these categories are having some personality disorders mainly. As we, as human beings, tend to get a victim of a thing very soon, and people are looking for preying others. These days' persuasion is big business, and most people are using it. The politicians, public speakers, leaders, and even media is focused on controlling the mind of others. But some people are manipulating you as they are manipulating others by using different love bombing techniques or by insulting them to make guilty for their decisions.

The cults can change your mind in such a way that you will forget about your earlier thoughts and try to stick to new ones. The same happens in the brainwashing, which may be used by terrorist groups or by the army for a prisoner. Dark hypnosis also is being used for verbal and nonverbal suggestions to a target for changing his point of view. Neuro-linguistic programing in the dark plays a crucial role as it can be used to change your mind and others for taking advantage. Now you have an exposure to mind control techniques including brainwashing, hypnotism, dark persuasion, manipulation, and neuro-linguistic programming. The purpose of telling about Dark Psychology aspects in not pushing you in these, but to aware you so that you can tackle such people and situations in a better way. You can use various techniques to keep your mind focused on the subject and keeping your mind out of others' control. Emotional intelligence is considered one of the best things that can be used to control your emotions as well as others. You will be aware of a saying that knowing something is never too late; it just requires constant study and practice. So no matter how old you are, you can still take up EI and make it better and healthier for the rest of your life. By improving your emotional intelligence, you will overcome dark aspects of others psychology.

Part 2 : How to Analyze People

Introduction

Modern science has proven that every individual's fundamental features are indelibly etched in the form of his body, head, face, and hands— an X-ray through which you can read the characteristics of any person on sight.

To any individual, in the world, the essential thing is to understand himself. The next one is to have the other fellow understand.

As long as you live in a civilized or densely populated society, you still need to consider your nature and other people's natures. No matter what you want from life, the desires, goals, and actions of other people are crucial obstacles in your path. Without the support, confidence, and comradeship of other men and women, you'll never get far. People rarely saw each other in primitive times and had far less to do with each other. The human element wasn't the primary problem then. Their environmental issues had to do with such things as the elements, violent storms, extremes of heat and cold, darkness, the ever-present threat of wild animals whose flesh was their food, yet who would eat them first unless they were quick in brain and body reflexes. But that has changed everything. Man has subjugated all other creatures, and now his supreme sovereign mold walks the earth. Until now, he's discovered and invented and built we live in skyscrapers, talk around the world without wires and turn darkness into daylight by pressing a button. To do this, our neighbors need to be better understood— to recognize that people differ from each other in their likes and dislikes, traits, talents, tendencies, and abilities. The combination of these makes it the nature of every person. It is not difficult to understand others because there always goes the corresponding physical makeup with each category of these traits— the externals by which the internal is usually indicated. This applies to all species on the globe and every subdivision within each species.

Learning to read men and women is a more enjoyable process than learning to read books, for every person you see is a true story, more romantic and absorbent than any person ever bound in coverings. Learning to read people is also a more straightforward process than learning to read books since the human alphabet includes fewer letters. Even though the man seems a mystifying mass of "funny little points" to the untrained eye, he isn't challenging to analyze now. This is because human feelings are, after all, but of a few kinds. There is some sort of hunger, love, hate, fear, hope, or ambition which gives rise to every human emotion and thought. Now our actions are according to our feelings. Each thinking, however transitory it may be, induces muscular activity, leaving its trace in that part of the physical organism which is closest to it. The second is to learn how to evaluate others to the end so that the relationship with them can be harmonious and mutually beneficial. Take individual according to how he was born, accept him as a mechanism, and deal with him in the manner appropriate to the device. Only in this way, and this, can you inspire or support others. You'll only be able to achieve real success in this way. Only in this way can you help your fellow find the work, the environment, and the marriage where he can be happy and prosperous. Look carefully at the people when analyzing them (but not stare fully). Don't leap to conclusions. As soon as we have made one, we humans have a perfect way to twist facts to fit our inference. But don't spend your time preparing to decide and forgetting, like the man who would jump a ditch. He ran so far back each time to get a good start, that when he got there, he never had the strength to climb. Gain a good start by observing.

The book, how to analyze people explores techniques for identifying and interpreting non-verbal language and using it to your benefit. It will teach you how a better understanding of the unconscious language will give you the power you need in everyday situations. With this book, you can reliably understand what makes someone when they do the things they do, only by reading what their unconscious movements are trying to say. By knowing what nonverbal actions mean, you'd be able to decipher hints that would lead you to know more about the people around you. At the same time, this book will also let you know how you can strengthen your relationship with others by learning how to communicate through the right non-verbal gestures better.

Chapter 1: Basics of Analyzing People

How do you read a human being? How can you quickly determine an individual without getting a ten-year psychology degree? For a human, that can be the hardest thing to do. You have to understand who you are as a human being and who others are. Comprehend your as well as others' likes, dislikes, etc. You've won over 1/2 of the fight if you can understand yourself and others. All of us are different, but we are all related as well. We are all human beings. We all have essential needs. We are members of the social order. Five human motivational needs hierarchy arranged by an upward order of importance, developed by Abraham Maslow are (1) physiological, (2) security, (3) social, (4) self-realization, and (5) self-realization. The only motivators are the unmet needs. The next step appears as a motivator once a need is satisfied. When you comprehend a person's basic needs, you can understand the person better. Pay attention to a person's nature. We are all the same as mentioned earlier, but different. What kind of person are you trying to analyze? How do you determine the life of a person? Beware of what that person does. What somebody does with their spare time will tell you all about their character? Does that person donate to charity? Entering the Church? Do they just go home and work? If someone in the community is active, it could mean that they care about the city, or it could mean that they're all about social status. You should ask yourself a couple of questions to find out which is true. Example questions that you might ask: What motivates this person to do so? Has he or she grown up within the community? Does it have an active social life? Does that person need anything? You can come up with a conclusion when you ask yourself those questions. Sometimes when someone does something else, it is because their culture is different from yours.

It is essential to pay attention to where they come from when you try to examine others. You can also have a good idea about what their "normal" behavior is if you know a little more about where a person is from. What is it about the nature of that person? Are they doing things right for the better? And does he always seem contrary to the person? A cynical person is somebody who usually feels missing somewhere. If our basic needs are not met, we can react to that in several different ways. One is by being cynical. Pay attention to how general a person is. We have positive people, negative people, and just sit in the middle of some people. Is that person a loner, or do they contribute to a particular crowd? If a person interacts with a specific type of group, it is likely for a cause that they feel comfortable in that crowd. We have a propensity to like people possessing same traits. If a person is associated with multiple different crowd types, you can assume that a person is an all-around person, with an open mind. Most open-minded people are empathic and have "been there and done it." If a person is inward and does not associate with crowds, they are unlikely to feel the need to associate with other people. Why wouldn't a person want to associate with others? That may be due to several factors. One explanation for this is that a person may not feel like they belong to others. Another reason could be from social fear. There are several other reasons a person could withdraw from socializing themselves.

1.1 Why is there a Need to Analyze People?

Human nature refers to a collection of intrinsic properties that all human beings share. The first step is to know why the person is being analyzed. As in a therapeutic way, are you analyzing them to help them? Analyze them so you can hire them? Analyze them to see if they're fit as a friend or a lover? What purpose will that analysis serve? Human behavior is incredibly unpredictable. In conduct, we cannot presume one fixed behavior pattern. Lavitt categorized behavior as: (i) Caused reaction, (ii) Motivated act, (iii) Goal-oriented behavior. One can conclude from these findings that action is a dependent factor. Through knowing measures, one can predict, steer, alter, and regulate person or group behavior. There are usually four fundamental premises concerning people's nature: individual differences, a whole person, induced actions (motivation), and personal value (human dignity).

The ability to understand others helps us anticipate what people might feel in a given situation, but it also gives us a sense of how people react. Social cognition is our ability to understand others, and it helps us to anticipate their actions and share experiences with others. It's also critical to understand the many nuances that underpin everyday speech because people often mean something other than what they say. For example, "it's hot in here" could be a statement of fact or a request to open a window. We need to guess the intention behind her remark, to understand the speaker. Social cognition can be a specific collection of abilities in the brain that are different from those required for non-social activities, such as the perception of a car being out of fuel. If so, it follows that even when non-social abilities remain intact, social cognition can be vulnerable to brain disorders. Social cognition involves you being able to identify other people's mental states by putting yourself in the shoes of someone else. This helps us understand their beliefs, their feelings, their experiences, and their intentions. From another point of view, we can offer empathy and think about things. It also allows us to move flexibly from our perspective to that of another. Ironically, social cognition is based on information that cannot be directly observed but is to be inferred from incoming knowledge and our social world experience. Yet research increasingly indicates that social cognition requires imitation by imitating the interactions of others as a way of understanding them.

1.2 Importance of Analyzing People

Analyzing someone means being able to empathize with that person, being able to think along the same lines as that person, being able to reason out what happened in someone's mind before doing what he/she did. When we meet someone, we start an empty file for them in our minds. And as we keep communicating with them, we define them slowly, perform complex calculations, and rough a profile on that file. We're calling it an' impression.' We describe our connection to them using the understanding as a reference. The idea is initially simple and easily malleable-you see, it's just a tiny script. But as we get to know our subject better and better, the file is growing more substantial, and calculations are becoming increasingly complicated, so our perception is set. By this time, we have' understood' our subject almost, if not entirely. Human beings can predict people's actions close to them-to predict what they would do in the light of a specific scenario. There could be a lot of' either-error involved in that process. But when they do anything out of the possibilities of guessing, it instantly puts us uncomfortable. My take is that if it continues to be like that, then the discomfort slowly turns into contempt, and then into hatred. Fights break out as people no longer' comprehend' one another.

Why is personality comprehensible? Well, it's just... well interesting from an academic perspective. Oh, but it's so much more than that from a life perspective. The more we understand ourselves and other people, the more we are going to be successful in dealing with people and situations; and get it right. Psychology may be an academic discipline, but it's a much more practical subject to understand personality. It's about using psychology to your advantage in everyday situations,' getting' people, influencing, helping and supporting people, getting your point across in a way that's right for you. It is a discipline of better understanding and shaping decision-making, motivating and managing people, and dealing with conflict and most hindrances. So sometimes it's important to distinguish between' psychology,' the subject, and' subjects,' that is to say the rest of us with all of our quirks and idiosyncrasies. And like all other techniques, the use of the Character Analysis can help as it breaks down the elements into measurable conditions. Does anyone first tend to hold back and think it through, or' talk out loud? Do they show a blunt directness or a wise, diplomatic approach? Do they want to get the job done before it chills, or do they get the job done freezing then? And sometimes, of course, you are going to get it wrong, we all do. That person that you described as an Extravert because they were so articulate and lucid was an Introvert who had been asked a question about something important to them, thought about it, and went for it. But that is all part of the learning process. We're all applied psychologists: we've got friends, we're going down the pub, we're going to parties, we're part of teams, and we're making people decisions all the time, and it's often incorrect. So let's start getting it right, it is far more rewarding.

When you're trying to understand other people, trying to put yourself in their shoes helps. Think about how you'd react if someone said that to you before you do something. Treat others the way they want you to treat them. Don't judge people until you think of their standpoint? You must be able to see the point of view of others, to better understand yours. Sometimes you need to see the flaws in yours from a fresh perspective. Occasionally, though, seeing the viewpoint of someone else will inspire yours too. Understanding the point of view of others will allow you to socialize, empathize, and rhetorically get better appropriately. It will enable you to be more empathetic when you see others' points of view. It improves both your life and the life with which you interact. It helps you by making you think about others by giving them a fair chance to help others. Any information or learning about this topic will help one understand empathy as well. Compassion means awareness and understanding, so to speak, of where another person comes from. And you cannot help but become a better person with that knowledge. It's just listening that is most important. Taking a step back from yourself and experiences is an acquired talent you will practice. You should try to put yourself in their shoes, and think from their point of view. In your mind, you can replay the incident putting yourself in the role of the other person. How the conversation could have gone differently, can you say?

The value of seeing the situation from another person's point of view will allow us to solve the problems more quickly and help the person who has the problem. It might also help us to learn about our family and friendship and to understand ourselves better. We should understand how the other person feels when they tell us about the problem. Through our point of view, when we see things, it's difficult to know how the other person feels and how they respond. We also get to learn about their experience, and we can see the perspective of the question they are experiencing. All the individuals want to be heard and understood. We are always arguing from our point of view to get the other person to see our way through things. When we do this all the time, we can reflect on the point of view of the other person, but no one would feel comprehended. Sometimes it takes an effort to see another person's view of the situation. We can understand what the concerns of the individual are, but we cannot know how they feel.

It's nice to see the situation from another person's point of view as it makes us see something we may not have known. This helps us to understand what the individual thinks about or what it means. We don't always have to be correct to know something by looking at the other person's point of view. When we open up ourselves, we would be a better person. Most of the people will listen and try to support us with our problems. This helps to save other people's disputes.

1.3 Benefits of analyzing people

According to Kohut (2013), personality is not a clearly defined and calculated concept; thus, we have developed implicit personality theories by studying the behavior of others and witnessing social interactions to understand ourselves and others (Maltby, Day & Macaskill, 2010). It is also evident, however, that individual differences exist, making personality analysis more complicated and one that is highly influenced by subjectivity and dependent upon it. This poses problems with understanding others accurately and also raises new concerns as to whether researching personality helps us to understand ourselves better than others. Allport (1955), communicates personality as a "becoming" phase, unique to each individual and their history, and believes that individual differences are made significant through comparison with agreed concepts. So it would make sense for many personality research theories to be based on common sense and rely heavily on intuition, often without explicit knowledge. Besides, psychological study (within personality psychology and other areas) is often influenced directly by personal experience. Allport also commented that we are then able to gather organized information about other people by understanding ourselves and recognizing problems that are relevant to our own experience. Empirical research by Chiu, Hong, and Dweck (1997) showed that an individual's perception of himself affects his view of others' personalities through pattern projection, and that shapes implicit theories of personality. This means that we have an inherent, more in-depth knowledge of ourselves and that as we grow this, we are also developing ideas about other people's actions around us that allow us to understand them.

All of us can agree to be idiots and behave as if our way is the right way, but if you believe that, you are naive if not blatantly stupid. Remember this one simple fact: there is no path, no specific direction, or a perfect or full train of thought. We are characterized by our differences and are there for us. We are all fractals of a whole, and as such, we should understand or at least try each other.

One benefit of being compassionate is that it exposes you to a lot of new viewpoints. With those viewpoints, life can be much more beautiful than you can imagine if you choose the right ones. Note that late people still seem to focus on the negative and not constructive viewpoints. Yet they do have issues with this sometimes. That's why they know which aspects are more relevant to you by comparison. And the more liberal views you are exposed to, the more empathy you will have and all viewpoints, even those with which you do not necessarily agree. That, in effect, also makes you a more compassionate person at the same time a most friendly person. We like someone who is still patient. Comprehension has introduced me to some of the most beautiful people. Even if they don't see the beauty inside. Some people have developed some long-lasting, meaningful connections with the people that they now call friends, even some relatives. Once friends get the right ones into your life, they can also enrich your quality of life. Good people attract good people, even within what some would deem the wrong crowd. When someone says good people, they talk about the individual's personality. You, too, can gain wisdom through understanding. You can do many things with this. Real knowledge comes with genuine understanding. Through this experience, you will guide people when they need to in the right direction. Whether it's friends, family, and so on. Learning opens the door to make you a better person. If we could all just sit down, be honest, and practice what is most essential within us: the ability to understand and help our fellow brothers and sisters in this insane thing we call life.

1.4 Speed Reading

Whether you're reading your supervisor, co-worker, or partner to understand people you have to give up prejudices properly, some barriers have to come down. It seems almost unbelievable to be able to read someone better than a poker pro and to uncover their lies and lessons. However, if you're prepared to keep an open mind, it's a skill you can build-literally. Body language interpretation is key to successful social interactions. Body language is an integral part of the way we interact with others. Nonetheless, most of us have, at best only intuitive knowledge of non-verbal communication. Luckily, if interpreting body language doesn't come to you quickly, or if you just want to get better at it, there is a tremendous amount of work that explains what the body is saying. You will develop a strong foundation in speed reading people rather than spending your time learning hundreds of nonverbal body language signs. Your first job is to keep the other person-centered. If you want to cause a spark with them, this needs to happen. Conversations sometimes go well, and sometimes they do not. Nonetheless, there is an array of messages in the body language that your mind can theoretically interpret. Yet investing a lot of time to see them actively will ruin the conversation before it's even begun. Do not just speak to someone the next time you're in a discussion as your brain tries to check every move they make secretly. This is as slow as reading a script and blocks your ability to sense the significant signals your body subconsciously sends you.

Keep it quick. Regard their big gestures, not the minor ones, rather than missing the whole series. If they're dying of boredom silently–a lack of eye contact, crossed arms, or running off their legs (trying to escape!)–it should be clear. Always, you should be careful with positive signals: nodding, laughing, and eye contact. Do not waste time trying to determine whether they play with their hair. They're drawn to you or scratch their nose because they're thinking about it. It's easy to misunderstand, and they're just getting an itch. Body language comparisons mainly work for your subconscious mind. You will eventually experience' The Law of Reverse Impact' when you push your conscious mind to step in and do something that your unconscious mind manages.

In other words, when you consciously start searching for signs to decipher, you're going to overthink things and trip your subconscious. It results in the talk being entangled in the tongue or being distant. The best thing to do is let your unconscious mind do what it's programmed to do–help you trust your gut instinct. Finally, you find a balance; you know the signs without worrying about what they say. This becomes instinctive.

Did you know that real science is based on instinct? Your hollow organs (e.g., your intestines) have nerve fibers that function as a second brain, which sends signals to your brain. That's why the word 'strong instinct.' It's the way your mind accesses an influx of extra information from another part of your body when you're following your intuition. One way to help our intuition understand others' speed up is to be at peace with discomfort. The earlier in awkward situations, you are relaxed, the easier it will be to get through any moments of tension.

Breathing slowly is an excellent tool for that. Your breath is connected to the prefrontal cortex with fibers hooked to the amygdala (an almond-shaped gray matter mass deep within each cerebral hemisphere). Reflect on the simple exercise of respiring peacefully through your nose and through your mouth. It shuts off your body's panic button and calms you down, so you can become more attuned to people reading. Persons are sometimes guarded, and their poker faces are preserved. Experienced negotiators and salespeople are typically good at this. Shake them out of this action by doing something unforeseen: it will often confuse them long enough to elicit a genuine response.

Chapter 2: Analyzing People through Body Language

Body language reading is a little like getting a superpower. People are mostly focused on the words the other person is using while talking to one another. Yet our bodies show how in ways we may not even know we feel. You can rock slightly, rub your lips with your finger, or play with your hair if you're nervous. And yeah, sometimes it feels like you've got a gift, but it's not an inborn talent-it's an ability that's acquired. There are many factors to consider when decoding body language. Culture and meaning, like "clusters," are significant. In body language, a cluster is two or more forms of movement that a person makes at about the same time. It can be a little easier to move through the world when you are more aware of the body language cues you are sending off. In a job interview, when the interviewer is talking, you can lean forward, keep your hands visible by following them on the table and keep your feet flat on the floor. If you'd like to seem more open at a group or bar, don't huddle in the corner and avoid eye contact. Instead, be more open and welcoming by looking at the room and having your back to the wall or the counter. Also, body language can be really important when it comes to customer service. Say you missed your flight, and you're at the airport, hoping the airline will rebook you for free on the next trip. Make sure you're in the right mindset before you hit the counter because your non-verbal gestures will show that. Calm down, relax your shoulders, as you put your hands on the desk, and make sure you confirm the natural curvature of your fingers.

2.1 Reading Body Language

Body language is a type of nonverbal communication in which physical actions are used to communicate or transmit the information, as opposed to words. This behavior includes facial expressions, positioning of the body, emotions, and movement of the hand, touch, and the use of space. Body language should not be confused with sign language, because sign languages are complete languages. Like, spoken words and they have their complex grammar structures, as well as being able to demonstrate the fundamental properties that occur in all languages. On the other hand, body language does not have a grammar structure. It must be interpreted generally, rather than having an absolute meaning that corresponds to an individual expression, so it is not a language like sign language. It is simply called a "language" because of popular culture. There are agreed-upon definitions of specific behavior within a culture. Interpretations may vary from one country to another, or learning to another. On this topic, there is debate about the universality of body language. Body language, a type of nonverbal communication, complements social interaction through verbal communication. Indeed some researchers conclude that nonverbal contact accounts for most of the information exchanged during interpersonal interactions. This helps build relationships between two people and controls contact but can be unclear.

The body language of the people around you speaks volumes, whether at the workplace or out with friends. It was suggested that body language is more than 60% of what we communicate, so learning to read the nonverbal signals that people send is a valuable skill. Body language shows what a person is thinking from eye expression to the direction a person points his or her feet in. Below are useful tips to help you learn how to read body language and understand the people you are communicating with better.

Studying Eyes

Behavior with your eyes can be very revealing. If speaking with someone, be alert whether he or she is making direct eye contact or looking away. The inability to make direct contact with the eye can mean boredom, disinterest, or even deception–particularly when somebody looks away and sideways. In comparison, when a person looks down, it often suggests nervousness or submissiveness. Search also for dilated pupils to decide whether someone is reacting favorably to you. As cognitive activity rises, pupils dilate, so if someone is concentrating on someone or something they want, their pupils will dilate automatically. Pupil dilation can be painful to detect, but you should be able to detect it under the right conditions. The blinking rate of a human can also speak volumes about what's going on inside. The risk of blindness rises when people think more or are anxious.

In some cases, a higher blinking rate indicates lying –particularly when accompanied by touching the face (especially the mouth and eyes). To look at something can mean a desire for that object. For instance, if somebody looks at the door, this might mean a desire to leave. Looking at a person may signify a desire to converse with him or her. As far as eye behavior is concerned, it is also implied that looking upwards and right during the conversation suggests a lie has been revealed while looking upwards means the person telling the truth. The explanation for this is that when people use their imagination to concoct a plot, they look up and to the right when they remember an actual memory.

Gazing the Face – Smiling

Even though people are more likely to monitor their facial expressions, if you pay close attention, you can still pick up valuable nonverbal clues. When trying to interpret nonverbal actions to pay particular attention to the ears. A simple technique for attracting body language smiles can be a useful gesture. Smiling is an important nonverbal cue to look out for. There are various kinds of smiles, including genuine laughs and fake smiles. A genuine smile embraces the whole face, while a fake smile uses only the lips. A genuine smile indicates the person is happy, and the people around him or she is enjoying the company.

On the other hand, a fake smile is meant to convey happiness or acceptance but indicates that the smile feels something else in reality. Another typical facial activity that includes only one side of the mouth and reveals sarcasm or confusion is a "half-smile" You may also note a slight grimace before someone smiles, which lasts less than a second. This usually implies that the person behind a fake smile is hiding his or her disappointment. Tight, pursed lips often suggest discontent while a relaxed mouth shows a carefree attitude and optimistic mood. An example of deception can be to cover the mouth or brush the lips with hands or fingers while speaking.

Proximity

Proximity is the distance from yourself to the other person. Keep an eye on how close someone stands or sits next to you to decide if they regard you favorably. Perhaps one of the best relationship markers is standing or sitting close to someone. On the other side, as you move closer, if someone backs up or moves away, this could be an indication that the relationship is not reciprocal. You can tell a lot about the kind of relationship that two people have just by looking at the closeness between them. Keep in mind that during contact, some societies prefer less or more space, so proximity is not always an accurate indicator of someone's affinity.

Mirroring

Mirroring means imitating the body language of the other person. Test to see if the person mirrors your behavior when communicating with someone. For example, if you sit with someone at a table and rest on the table with an elbow, wait 10 seconds to see if the other person is doing the same. A further that mirroring movement includes simultaneously taking a sip of a drink. If someone imitates your body language, it's a perfect sign he or she is trying to establish a friendship with you. Try to change the body posture and see if the other person makes similar changes to theirs.

Observing the Head Movement

The pace at which a person nods his or her head when you speak indicates his or her tolerance-or lack. Slow nodding means the person is interested in what you say and wants you to keep talking. Quick nodding implies that the person has heard enough and that he wants you to finish speaking or give him or her a speech turn. Throughout the conversation, tilting the head sideways can be a sign of curiosity in what the other person says. Holding the head down can be a sign of doubt or confusion. We often point at what they are interested in or share a bond with the head or face. You can say in groups and gatherings which the influential people are based upon how much people look at them. The less critical individuals, on the other hand, are looked at less frequently.

Observing the Feet of a Person

The feet are a part of the body where people sometimes "leak" essential nonverbal signals. The reason people transmit nonverbal cues accidentally via their feet is that they are typically so focused on managing their facial expressions and positioning of the upper body that important clues are exposed via the feet. When standing or sitting, a person usually points his or her feet in the direction they wish to go. So if you find that somebody's feet are looking in your path that may be a good indication that they have a favorable opinion of you. What refers to one-on-one interaction and interaction between classes? In reality, you can tell a lot about group dynamics just by observing the body language of the people involved, especially the way they point their feet. Furthermore, if someone seems to be engaging in conversation with you, but their feet point in someone else's direction, it's possible that he or she would rather speak to that person (regardless of whether the upper body signs indicate otherwise).

Watching Hands Signals

As with the feet, when looking at a body language, the hands leak essential nonverbal signals. This is an important tip, so pay close attention to this next section when interpreting the body language. Observe hands in body language while standing in pockets. Look for similar hand signals, like the other person putting their hands in their pockets or hands on their heads. This can mean anything from nervousness to total disappointment. Unconscious pointing can also speak volumes, demonstrated by hand gestures. An individual should point in the general direction of the person with whom they share a connection when making hand gestures (these nonverbal signals are particularly relevant to watch for during meetings and when engaging in groups). Supporting the head with the hand by leaning on the table with an elbow may mean that the person is listening and still holding the crown for emphasis. Boredom can be demonstrated by supporting the head with both elbows on the bed, on the other side. When a person holds an item between him or her and the person with whom they communicate, this acts as a shield designed to block the other person out. For instance, if two people speak, and one person holds a pad of paper in front of him or her, this is called a nonverbal communication blocking act.

Examine the Position of Arms

Think of the arms of a human as the gateway to both body and self. If a person crosses his or her sleeves when communicating with you, this is typically seen as a protective move that blocks them. In addition, crossed arms may signify fear, weakness, or a closed mind. If a genuine smile and overall comfortable stance accompany crossed arms, then it may suggest a confident, relaxed attitude. When someone puts their hands on their hips, they are usually used to assert dominance and are used more often by men than by women. The tips above may give you insight into the real motives behind people's behavior, but they are not foolproof. Bear in mind when studying body language that these strategies will not apply 100 percent of the time to all people. To correctly interpret nonverbal signals, other factors such as culture and the general body language patterns of an individual have to be taken into account.

2.2 Positive and Negative Gestures

Although learning the body language is not as simple as some television shows, when dealing with clients and business partners, it is still a useful and necessary ability. This chapter discusses the universal nature of body language, why much of it is comprehensive, and how this can help communicate even when two people do not share the same vocabulary. At different times people exhibit both positive and negative body language. Nevertheless, not every physical action which a person performs is inherently an example of body language. Although getting your arms crossed is an indication of negative body language, it could just as well be a sign of cold feeling.

In addition, don't depend on certain behaviors as body language indicators; it's also more useful to get an idea of the general practice of the individual. The more you learn about the person ahead of time, the easier their body language seems to decipher. Body language is best demonstrated by the amount of personal space between you and the other person. This is usually a sign of negative body language if the person keeps his distance. But, if the person leans in and makes a lot of eye contact while talking to you, these can be taken as indicators of positive body language. The reason people want to understand body language is not to obtain somebody's knowledge, but to understand their feelings and how they feel. Through knowing the sentiments of the other person, you can get a better sense of who they are, and as a result, have greater control over the conversation.

Positive Gestures

Positive gestures can be described as those nonverbal movements and gestures that express interest, excitement, and positive reactions to what is being said by others.
Whether you interact with your body is critical, as research shows that 60 to 90 percent is nonverbal. To many, body language is known as the most crucial aspect of communication, as it sends signs about how we really feel.
When we see or hear something useful, or at least interpret it as positive, we may do what is known as the positive movements of evaluation. In this chapter, we are not going to talk about the everyday positive appraisal movements like smiling, intense eye contact, clapping, etc. But the emphasis will be on the lesser-known gestures you'll probably miss or forget if you don't know what they mean.

Eye Brow Rubbing

When someone sees something they like, they rub off one of their eyebrows along the entire length of the forehead with their index finger from end to end. The rubbing motion consists of a single or a double movement, which starts near the nose from the inner corner of the brow and ends at the outer edge.
It's as if the eyebrows of the person are so high that the brow's hair is falling on their eyes and blocking the view of the beautiful thing they're looking at. So they have to brush the inexistent eyebrow hair aside to see the object clearly, just as a girl would push her hair away from her face when it stops her

from seeing it clearly. This is a simple mnemonic for recalling the gesture's significance. Often this gesture can happen very quickly, like in a flash, as soon as a person testifies to something positive. If somebody makes this gesture as soon as they meet you, they know they like you, or at least they're interested in what you have to show them or tell them.

Fixing Eye Glasses

When a person wears glasses, the action mentioned above of' rubbing the brow' is difficult, if not impossible, to perform. Changes in body language occur in real-time, and when a person wearing glasses sees something positive, you shouldn't expect him to take his spectacles out, fold them on the table, then rub his eyebrow, and then ritualize his glasses back on. That is too long a process, and mostly spontaneous involuntary responses are expressions of body language. So the person has to use some other gesture that can express the same' good appraisal' message and something that requires some different kind of' clearing the vision.' When a person wearing glasses sees something interesting, he changes his glasses to take a better look at the thing he is looking at with his one or both hands. Every time, the' eyebrow rubbing' gesture is an individual gesture with the same meaning, and you will get accurate results even if you forget the context. But you need to be a little careful when it comes to the' adjusting glasses ' gesture. The person's glasses may be uncomfortable, and so he has to re-adjust them. But if a friend of yours changes his glasses as soon as a pretty girl checks into the room, then you know that his glasses were not uncomfortable, mainly if after' clearing his vision' he doesn't stop staring at her.

The Face Platter

The females do this movement exclusively. It is more of a symbol of female courtship than a substantive act of appraisal. It is common sense that a person is not sending out signals of interest to those they don't see positively. So it's a kind of tacit constructive act of appraisal. When a girl is talking to a guy she's' evaluating positively,' she may rest her face on her hands, flattened one above the other, like a platter. She's putting her face, her crowning charm, on a plate to admire the guy just like tea is served on a shelf to guests. She's asking the man non-verbally,' Take a good look at my face here and be floored.' It is sometimes performed with only one hand, in a fist-like position with fingers and spread out under the nose.

Negative Body Gestures

Negative body language is either a deliberate manifestation of negative feelings by body movements or an involuntary one. Being able to notice negative body language may help one with personal or professional relationships, and understanding when another is upset or disappointed. If one wants to leave a good impression on an audience or listener, it can help to know what negative body language to avoid. Body language can be even more important than the words spoken. There's a lot of apparent motions people do when they hear or see things they don't like, like closing their eyes, turning their heads to look away, wrinkling their nose in disgust, etc. Then there is the ' nose brush ' that is not so clear that it is easily missed or ignored.

Touching Nose

If a person finds himself in a position that he does not like or' consider negatively,' you might catch him doing the classic sign of negative assessment-the nose brush. The nose touch ranges from rubbing the nose ridge to scratching it, gripping it, or even touching the nostrils underneath the nose. This movement is experienced when a person feels self-conscious, frustrated, or nervous. This movement is often seen in liars as they lie or are about to rest. In fact, it became known as the' Pinocchio effect' as the biological mechanism that causes the individual to rub his nose this way. We are slightly stressed when we lie deliberately, our blood pressure rises and inflates the nose, which causes the nerve endings to tingle in the trunk, causing us to rub it to relieve the sensation. You may see this movement in a person who is self-conscious when he enters a public place. If a person says something embarrassing about himself or hears someone else saying something awkward about him, you can see him in a quick motion rubbing his nose. Yet, by far, the best thing about this gesture is that a very high degree of precision will help you spot lies.

Bad Pose

This is one of the types of negative body language which is more ignored. You may think the lousy posture contributes only to physical problems. Incorrect. The truth is terrible posture often impacts the mood, stress levels, and self-esteem negatively. Drooped shoulders will make you look and feel tired and weaker than you are.

Poor Feet and Legs Position

Whenever you are sitting, your legs and feet that send messages you don't even know about. The gap between your legs and knees will tell you something about your personality. If your knees are all together and your feet apart, you might come off as childish insecure. You may look defensive, remote, or even narrow-minded by crossing your legs. And then, there is a spread of man. Holding the legs far apart shows a degree of superiority. But it can also show arrogance and, in formal situations, it is often unacceptable. And even if your legs are not too close or far apart, the fault maybe your feet. Foot moves are a significant' tale' we are often unaware of. The more you tap your feet on the floor, or go up and down, the more likely you are to show anxiety and nerves.

Arms Crossed

The thing with crossed arms is-like having an X symbol to protect yourself in children's games-they make you look defensive. Anyone communicates with you may find you unimpressed or uninterested with what they tell you. Yet crossing your arms doesn't necessarily make you look approachable.

Weak Position of Fingers and Hands

There are several things you can do with your hands and fingers, which represent the language of the negative body. Next, your palms are clasped in. It's a collective action for people when they feel stressed, but when you do business with others, it's counterproductive, and you're expected to project self-assurance. First, you keep your hands behind the back or in your pockets. It may be a role most of us take subconsciously, but it puts you in danger of behaving like something you're hiding. Often, rubbing your hands when sitting down is not pleasant, or pressing the fingers of one side over the other to form a "steeple." Such movements can be associated with being deceitful or intimidating.

Hand Shakes

Handshakes aren't easy to master. Unfortunately, one of the more extreme types of negative body language is a weak or overly firm handshake. Particularly when there are first impressions on the track. Soft handshakes are considered vulnerable because they require sweaty hands or cold hands or hands that barely come into contact with the palm of the other. We can paint a picture of someone who lacks both authority and confidence. Perhaps they mean someone who, in fact, is just cold. Whereas handshakes are considered too heavy with too much intensity and make you come off as violent.

Little Eye Contacts

Some things to say about eye contact. In many different ways, too small of it means bad news: you're acting unprofessional, you're inexperienced, you're nervous, or you're insincere with others. It can seriously hurt you at a party or during a date, right off the bat. There is a reason that we, like children, are taught to look people in the eye when talking or listening. This makes them feel at ease with you and happy. Too much eye contact causes the opposite effect. It might make one look rude, arrogant, or aggressive.

2.3 Importance of Body Language

In this highly competitive environment, the body language is of utmost importance. The corporate sector values the right body language a lot, and any signs of bad body language will interrupt agreements, even resulting in people losing the network. An adage says, "Actions speak louder than words." Our body postures, along with their gestures and positioning different parts of the body, play an essential role in bringing out our feelings and emotions, even if we don't consciously express the feelings.

Across today's society, body language plays multiple functions. Despite the advances in technology, this means of communication is seen as obsolete and cannot be relied on. Something people should not forget, though, is that this means that they are part of the most direct means of communication before other means can be put in place. People who lack a shared communicative language find it difficult to communicate with each other. The only quick way to do this is by using body language. In normal circumstances of life, emotions find their origins in body language, and the twisting of some parts of the body can turn out to communicate a strong message to the target recipient. People around the globe love the style of the body, and the positions it plays. Body language produces concepts for creating the most advanced means of communication. What is most critical is to understand the communication philosophy which scientists are to achieve. Keeping faith in uncompromising innovations makes people forget that our bodies are the practical means, and the only challenge is to learn how to use them. Mastering Body

Language is one of the most exciting things one can do, and it turns out to be more of a pleasure in most cases.

2.4 Importance of Body Language in the Workplace

Before you even say a word, your body language speaks volumes to you. Just by looking at their facial expressions and actions, everybody forms opinions about people. It's only average and extends to everyone. As discussed earlier, body language can be described in simple terms as the conscious and subconscious physical movements which reveal our true feelings and emotions. Body language plays an even more significant part of work. The expression "the first impression is the last impression" must have been understood. Candidates are judged based on their body motions and physical movements from the very beginning of job interviews.

Communication at work is essential to perform tasks and to work as a team. The phrases spoken by staff members are just a part of the puzzle of contact. Body language expresses the thoughts or intentions of one colleague. Such nonverbal clues are capable of aligning or overlapping with words coming out of his mouth. An understanding of your body language lets you determine the message your colleagues are sending.

Body language involves attitudes and behaviors. The eye contact is an indicator of body language in the workplace. Maintaining eye contact is an expression of value, focus, confidence, and integrity. Turning away from your gaze can cause a colleague to believe you're not honest. The general facial expressions at work reflect the thoughts about the situation as well. Your overall attitude also represents your confidence and interest in what you're doing. During a meeting slumping in your chair will lead others to feel that you are uncomfortable or not interested in the presentation. Hand gestures also play a role in contact within the workplace. Paying attention to the body language of a boss or supervisor will help you figure out how to go about it. Noting body language in a one-on-one or small-group scenario lets you discover a lack of confidence, an issue in an employee's current project, or even dishonesty. You may identify potential problems by analyzing the body language and find solutions for them. If an employee does not feel confident about a particular task, there is an opportunity for further training or assistance. When you thought a problem occurred with a project, you should focus on solving the problem.

Noting body language will say more than the words your workers can tell you so you can run the workplace better. You should gauge the body language of the audience to weigh how your message is viewed when giving a presentation or leading a conference. Employees may feel bored or disengaged by avoiding eye contact, fidgeting with items such as pens or notebooks, scribbling, or poor posture of the body. Employees who think defensive or disagree with your message are more likely to turn away, keep their arms crossed, or avoid contact with their eyes. You should switch gears to include the participants in a presentation or conference. When workers seem to disagree with your post, you should open the discussion to tackle the problem and come up with solutions together.

While body language can indicate the feelings of a colleague, misinterpretation of the body language may lead to confusion and tension. In a diverse environment, this may become more of an issue where cultural differences interpret the body language harder. If the body language of a colleague seems to show anger, dishonesty, irritation, or similar negative feelings, further examine before responding. Ask additional questions to get a sense of the actual message and thoughts from your colleague. The more they work together, the colleagues also get a better understanding of each other's body language.

Chapter 3: Analyzing People in Dating and Love

The body language can be an incredibly helpful device when you're out on a first date. If you don't pay attention to the non-verbal signs that your time is showing, you can often go on talking about something that makes them uncomfortable, or they may find it awkward. While you don't want to go into a date hiding who you are, you want to put your best foot forward, so if you're a decent match, you'll be able to bring up the riskier issues a little later if you like your date. It, of course, means paying close attention to the actions of your data, which can be challenging when you are to be charismatically speaking and listening to what they say.

Nonetheless, with a little practice, you'll get the hang of looking for the right signs and not have to spend a lot of time worrying about them. On a date, you are not looking for anything complicated— just the general symptoms of ease and discomfort that we discussed above. It indicates that you are only paying attention to how your date with their body is secured. Some people would initially be relatively well guarded. They should cross their heads, keep a reasonable distance, and keep their palms face-up. On a first date, this is all right and relatively common, and your goal is to make the body language something more open and welcoming. You will, of course, do this when you interact with them, but by doing it yourself, you will encourage free body language. We appear to imitate someone else's actions to some degree, so if you're warm and comfortable, it'll help change your date to suit your behavior. This means keeping your arms open and uncrossed, giving whenever possible and necessary a genuine smile, minimizing the distance from your time, and even exposing your palms. All these things mean you're relaxed and also will help make your date more confident.

You also want to be careful not to get yourself psyched out just because you have picked up some negative body language. Comfort levels frequently fluctuate on dates because, for most people, it is often a little nerve-wracking in the first place. Don't be afraid to make any mistakes. For a recital, as a piano teacher would advise you if you are playing a wrong note, you should just keep going. Notice the non-verbal signals to see how you are doing and concentrate on anything that offers a positive language for the body. If you get extended moments of negative body language, move on to a different topic. Of course, sometimes, you just won't click, and the date will be an uncomfortable evening full of negative, non-verbal signs. If this occurs, the same rule of piano-playing applies: don't get stuck on a problem — just move on.

3.1 Body Gestures in Dating and Love

Love is one of the most profound feelings human beings know. There are many kinds of love, but in a romantic relationship with a happy partner (or partners), many people seek its manifestation. For many, romantic relationships represent one of life's most significant aspects, providing a source of deep fulfillment. There seems to be an inherent need for human connection — but the ability to form safe, caring relationships is taught. Some evidence suggests that the ability to create a stable relationship starts to evolve in infancy, in the earliest encounters of a child with a caregiver who consistently meets the needs of the baby for food, treatment, comfort, security, stimulation, and social contact. These relationships are not inevitable but are theorized to create deeply ingrained patterns of other-related relationships. Failed relationships occur for many reasons, and a relationship breakdown is often a source of great psychological distress. Many people need to work actively to learn the skills required to make partnerships last and succeed.

Love and contact regularly maintain healthy relationships. While relationships can take several forms, it has been shown that specific characteristics are particularly important for healthy relations. For example, each person should feel confident that their partner actively devotes time and attention to each other. We must also both be committed to accepting the unavoidable disagreements and obstacles that occur. Good relationships in the 21st century are typically marked by a sense of fairness, both emotional and physical— particularly in the distribution of the chores necessary to maintain a household. Partners in strong relationships often feel grateful to each other, give and accept affection freely, and participate in frank gender discussions. In good relationships, partners tend to give the benefit of the doubt to their partner, which creates a sense of being in life on the same team. That feeling, which is sustained over the long term, will help couples resolve several challenges. Given that we can use straightforward body language cues in a dating and persuasion sense to determine what our partner is thinking. We will read whether his / her limbic system says to remain and snuggle, or cut and run. Such limbic system signals are especially crucial to romance, as that portion of our brain is also responsible for our love feelings.

Positive body language: If he or she likes what you are doing or asking, your partner may step towards you and decrease the space between you two. Alternatively, other loving actions may include: leaning in toward you, feet pointing toward you and wiggling happily, legs uncrossed and relaxed, arms open and palms up, playfully fondling jewelry or clothing, laughing, eye contact extended, or looking down shyly.

Negative body language: If your partner dislikes or asks what you are doing, your partner may move away from you and create space between you two. Moreover, other actions that indicate disdain include: staying away from you, feet pointing away from you, legs crossed and straight, arms crossed, palms down, hands closed, eyes itching, nose scratching, or neck rubbing, frowning, grimacing, and shifting your head to the side.

Check for variations of the above patterns (called clusters) when you are trying to figure out how your partner feels about you or your approach. Generally, when you see a few "positive" signals from the above list, you can bet that the limbic system of your partner is firing in the "right" direction, happy and loving. In general, they are positive about you and your actions towards them. By comparison, if you see a few "negative" signs from the above list, you can bet that the limbic system of your partner is firing in the "evil," unhappy, or confused direction. Use that data as feedback. Changing your behavior or waiting for a better mood may be a good idea. Paying attention to simple body language sign clusters can go a long way in the dating process. Use them to tell your partner what it feels like. For optimal results, choose your actions accordingly. Basically, you'll be more empathetic, more appealing, and more persuasive.

3.2 Truth and Relationship

Being in a relationship will come along with a great many questions. If you continue to see someone for the first time, you'll inquire if they like you back. You may wonder later whether they are looking for a serious relationship, or whether they believe in marriage or not, or what their family dynamic is like. However, if you wonder whether they love you or not, then you may be able to tell without even having to ask. Indeed, there are certain body language clues that your partner is in love with you that if you don't get the verbal confirmation you need, you might want to keep an eye out. That's not to suggest your friend shouldn't have their emotions verbalized. Hearing "I love you" in any relationship, is significant. But there are tons that we can tell from their body language about our friend, even if it isn't always the most read on-point. From the body language, you can say to a lot, but love is pretty complicated. "It's pretty hard to determine real love using body language.

One of the most important things to achieve a good and healthy relationship is to be honest in a contact that can be either a girlfriend/boyfriend or a married couple. Second, in a relationship telling the truth, it's a way to gain the other person's faith and trust in one another whenever they need it. For instance, if you're in trouble, you can tell your partner who's going to listen to you, and he'll let you know what to say. Second, you can believe the other person is not going to be dishonest towards you, which could bring a lot of benefits in the future, preventing regular disputes. You can believe that he/she can tell you if you're doing something wrong or irritating to your friend, so in the future, you'd be more vigilant. This is one of the reasons that we differ with people who think that rational lies are needed in a relationship, the easier it is to live with them, the more they say lies. If, after a few years, a couple keeps telling lies, all their conversation might turn around a lie at one point, so they might not know when they trust or not in what they're listening to. In a love relationship, in particular, it is essential to be completely honest before the marriage because this person could be the one you are living with for the rest of your life, and you need to know precisely how he/she is. No one wants to live with a liar.

It eliminates an excellent potential for anxiety when you know you can trust your mate to the fullest. It also builds up your protection so that not only do you feel good about your mate, but you feel better about life too. Getting an honest connection provides a sort of barrier between you and the world's difficulties. Finding a friend that you can trust and rely on also makes taking the chances that help us grow easier. Some people feel that little white lies are good, and in some cases, that's real, which may save their partner any grief. Yet you can't just sometime have a tradition of integrity in your relationship. When you choose to ignore or distort reality in order to make things look a little better, it might actually damage your link at heart. It can cause more confusion than it is worth trying to "cover" your partner or just try to avoid looking bad. Going overboard in all of your interactions is safest. If asked what attributes a partner wants, most people would mention "honesty" among them. Alas, most of us had the sense of being lied to. You need to know when you have a relationship and a family that everyone is on the same page, and this is hard to do unless both of you are honest. What honesty does offer you is a lot of comforts. Knowing you can trust your partner inherently helps you to be your best self and your relationship can continue to thrive because you can give each other the positive energy you need to handle the ups and downs of life.

Honesty doesn't just tell the truth, either. It's also about telling the truth in a way that will help your partner understand and benefit from it. Of course, we all want to hear how awesome we are, but we can also benefit from some slight adjustments to how we do things. This is where a little sincerity from someone you love and trust can help you make the small adjustments that can make a better place for your future. Honesty must be delicate in this situation. If you have to say something which may be disturbing to your loved one, do it as politely as you can. You need to be kind enough to answer your questions. If not, the post could be lost in an avalanche of hurtful feelings. You both will be able to communicate much more if your hearts aren't damaged in the process. Honesty is not just an action but a way of life. Holding it central in your relationship will bring more good and keep the negative things upside down. In an understanding, you can trust each other completely, which brings a type of freedom and security that makes your relationship work in the best possible way.

3.3 Male and Female Dating Signs

The trend of not defining a relationship is becoming increasingly common, and in the midst of this phenomenon, "dating" has become a catchall term for everything from hooking up to being in an intimate relationship, and that can make navigating an uncertain world. "Dating" is a word that becomes enormously complicated once you unpack it, and what that term means to any given person is mostly a matter of semantics, much like what a person means when they say they're "seeing someone" or "hanging out" or "having something."

Male Dating Signs

Note that most people in the early stages of a relationship are on their best behavior and unlikely to express blatantly sexist views (though surprisingly, many still do). Instead, sexist men frequently show in subtle ways negative beliefs about women, ones that are easy to miss at the early stages of excitement and romance. Some men hold views that they don't even know are sexist, as do some women, further complicating matters. For instance, a man who believes a woman should be protected, cared for, and respected may not seem sexist, except these men are unlikely to feel comfortable with a woman who out-earns them significantly. Some women may want a partner who supports them, cares about them and admires them. Still, they would probably also want the choice to be practical without creating anger, anxiety, and animosity to him. Most women would probably want to know if the guy they are dating is inherently sexist, and they should be informed by the following tips. Such signs should be considered, however, only as red flags or concerns that require more attention— not grounds for immediate condemnation. Many people may not have adequately thought about their behavior, and others may not be conscious of their behavior, or their views are troublesome. If your date shows any of these signals, it may be a good idea to ask them specifically about issues that concern you (e.g., whether they'd be comfortable with a woman who made more than they did, or whether they think it's okay for men to be equally involved in child-rearing or primary caregivers).

Signs That He is Sexist

1. He orders you to have a drink or meal without telling you to. When somebody tells you, they presume they know what's right for you or what you want. If your date is a professional mind reader with a dazzling Vegas of his own, he should always consult with you first. It might not be sexist if: he had previously mentioned his favorite drink/meal, and you indicated that you would be open to trying it. He should have consulted with you even then, but ideally, his unilateral action is more a sign of over-enthusiasm than a reflection of sexism.

2. He asks you questions about your goals to raise children but not about your career goals. In doing so, he believes you should be more motherhood-focused than your job. It might not be patriarchal if: you had previously explained your desire to be a stay-at-home mom if he spoke with equal enthusiasm about his role as a father or if he happily stated that his company gives paternity leave.

3. On a first date, he'll call you babe, sweetie, toots, or other pet names. Pet names should represent sentiments of love or

affection and should be received as such. If, after knowing you for all of two hours, he doles out pet names, it will more likely reflect feelings of superiority on his part.

4. If referring to a previous girlfriend or ex-wife, he resorts to calling names. Use derogatory terms about another woman when it's not just bad judgment on a date but also a reflection of his feelings towards women in general. If: he's getting over a nasty and recent divorce in which he suffered significant emotional or financial wounds, and you were the one who asked him (unwisely) about his ex, it might not be sexist. He's probably not ready for a new relationship anyway, so give this one a break.

5. He finds it necessary to express his "women's ideology." The fact that he even has a women's philosophy is a concern as it suggests that all women are similar and want the same things that smack of sexism even if his "beliefs" sound optimistic (for example, I think women should be placed on a pedestal!). It might not be sexist if: you asked him about his "women's" views, gave your argument about your men's opinions, or questioned an ex for the way women were viewed— prompting your date to point out that he is not "like that."

Note, if the man you are dating meets any of these requirements, then further consideration should be warranted, not immediate dismissal. It may also be a good idea to think about the differences between men and women through your own opinions and attitudes in order to assess if your personal values are sexist in some way. Having patriarchal views is typically a product of our culture and social context, so we might have such viewpoints, but if we take the time to think things over, our attitudes can and should be changed.

Female Dating Signs

Attraction comes in many delicate ways. As a guy, knowing these signs of attraction so you can enjoy them for your own sake, but also so you can rejoice and intensify, is your work. People who miss out on the signs of desire will miss other chances to interact with women who are interested in them. This sounds stupid, but when we take them out on field nights. He walks away disappointed because he doesn't know she was holding on to his every word, even though the signals are clear to the other coaches and to me.

Top Body Signs of Attraction

Preening is essentially one of the things that women do when they are around a man they are interested in "fixing herself." This is partially nerves. Part of it is that she does want to look after you better. Part of it is that there is just something sexy about a woman putting together herself, and people subconsciously know that.

She Laughs at Your Jokes

While it's true that women like a man who can make them laugh, it's worth noting that because you're the funniest guy at the bar, she might not laugh. She might just laugh because she loves you. Actually, it doesn't matter much to your ends. Either she thinks you're hilarious, which is fine, or she wants you to believe that she thinks you're curious, which might be even better. Beware of female laughter. It's a dead giveaway she loves your company, whether she thinks you're funny or not.

Eye Contact

When you're out in a bar, when a girl tries to get away from you, one of the easiest ways to do that is to start tossing her eyes around the room, searching for anything else she can do but talk to you. In contrast, the eyes are not all soul windows. They're kind of spirit tractor beams. Once she looks back at you, she tries to pull you in and prolong the conversation. Keep your eyes on her. It will not only help you build attraction, but it will also allow you to understand the attraction that she throws on you. This could be the only sign of attraction you'll get, especially with shy or reserved girls. Be on the screen, then.

Asking Personal Questions

Personal questions are a common sign that many people miss out on attraction. Talking about issues that go beyond the usual "getting to know you" forms of formalities that people feel they're going through when they meet someone new. Check for questions you're just asking others for when you're trying to get a sense of who they are. Alternatively, she could ask you questions of a more emotional nature to create more of a connection and relationship with you. If she asks you several questions, she probably isn't just looking for information. She is trying to keep interacting with her. Don't write off their curiosity in you as being "being friendly."

Touch

Girls are not touching those guys they are not interested in. This involves other' accidental' brushes. Men tend to initiate a variety of complex evolutionary reasons, while women tend to put on the brakes. What this means is that she probably won't do whilst you may initiate an overt touch. What she is trying to do, then, is touch you "accidentally." Do not read every accidental contact as a winning symbol. What you are looking for is not one example in isolation. What you're looking for is a pattern that repeats itself. When she continues to bang her elbow against yours in a completely empty room, she will be drawn to you. When, once in a place full of people, she brushes her arm against yours, she may well be in you, but she does not signify anything other than being in a crowded room. If she touches you, wonder why she does it. If there is no other real reason than desire, then intensify the connection. Begin with something small as touching her face, arms, or upper back and see where she's going from.

Chapter 4: Types of Personality

Personality, traditional way of thinking, feeling, and acting. Character includes moods, attitudes, and beliefs and is conveyed most clearly in relationships with other people. This involves both innate and acquired behavioral characteristics that differentiate one person from another and can be seen in people's links with the environment and the social group. Type of personality refers to the psychological classification of people of different types. Forms of nature are sometimes differentiated from character traits; the latter embodying a smaller class of behavioral characteristics. Models are sometimes said to include qualitative differences between people, while features could be interpreted as differences in quantities. For example, introverts and extroverts are two fundamentally distinct categories of people according to style theories. Introversion and extroversion are part of a continuous aspect, with many people at the center, according to trait theories. Existing typologies of personality expose and improve knowledge and understanding of individuals, as compared to declining knowledge and knowledge, as is the case with stereotyping. Suitable typologies can allow for improved ability to predict clinically relevant information about people and establish practical treatment approaches. There is detailed literature on the topic of classifying the various types of human behavior and equally thorough literature on personality traits and domains. These classification schemes aim to characterize typical temperament and personality and demonstrate the common features of different types of character and personality; they are primarily the domain of the psychology discipline. On the other hand, personality disorders mirror the practice of psychiatry, a medical specialty, and are disease-oriented.

The word personality is defined in many ways, but two primary significances have emerged as a psychological definition. The first concerns regarding apparent differences that exist between people: the study of personality in this context focuses on classifying and describing relatively stable psychological characteristics of humans. The second meaning emphasizes those qualities which make all people similar and distinguish cerebral man from other species; it guides the theorist of personality to look for those moderates among all people that explain the nature of man as well as the factors that influence the course of life. This duality may help to describe the two tracks and tendencies that personality researches have conducted. On the one hand, the study of ever more specific qualities in humans, and on the other, the quest for the structured totality of psychological functions that emphasize the interplay between organic and psychological events within humans and those social and biological events that surround them. Nevertheless, it should be noted that no concept of personality finds universal acceptance within the field.

Personality research can be said to derive from the fundamental idea that people are characterized by their characteristic individual behavior patterns— the distinctive ways in which they walk, speak, arrange their living quarters or communicate their desires. Any behavior, perinatologists — as those who are called to systematically research personality — examine how people differ in the way they express themselves, and try to determine the causes of these differences. While other psychological disciplines explore many of the same roles and processes, such as focus, perception, or motivation, the pulmonologist examines how these different processes work together and become incorporated to give each person a distinctive identity, or personality. The systematic psychological study of nature has originated from a variety of sources, including medical case studies focused on life in crisis, philosophy investigating man's existence, and biology, sociology, and social psychology.

4.1 Psychological Theories on Types of Personalities

The notion of individuals falling into specific categories of personality type about body characteristics has fascinated various contemporary psychologists as well as their counterparts among the ancients. Nevertheless, the idea that people have to fall into one or another static type of personality has been increasingly discarded. Two comprehensive collections of theories, the humoral and the morphological, are listed here.

Humoral Theories

Maybe the oldest known personality theory is found in the cosmological writings of the Greek philosopher, physiologist Empedocles, and physician Hippocrates which is relevant to speculations. The celestial elements of Empedocles — air (with its associated properties, warm and moist), earth (cold and dry), and fire (warm and dry), and water (cold and wet) — were linked to health and corresponded (in the above order) to the physical humors of Hippocrates, which were associated with temperament variations: blood (sanguine temperament), black bile (melancholic), yellow bile (choleric) and phlegm (phlegmatic). This theory has existed in some form for over 2,500 years, with its belief that temperament is determined by body chemistry. According to these early thinkers, both emotional stability and general health rely on an adequate balance between the four senses of humor of the body; an excess of one can create a particular body disorder or an excessive personality trait. Therefore, it would be expected that a person with an abundance of blood would have a sanguine temperament — that is, cheerful, enthusiastic, and excitable. Too much black bile (the dark blood may be combined with other secretions) was thought to create a melancholic temper. An oversupply of yellow bile (secreted by the liver) will lead to anger, irritability, and a view of life that is "jaundiced." An excess of phlegm (secreted in the respiratory passages) has been claimed to make people stolid, apathetic, and undemonstrative. When biological science advanced, these simplistic theories about body chemistry were replaced by more complex ideas, and by contemporary studies of hormones, neurotransmitters, and substances generated within the central nervous system, such as endorphins.

Morphological Theory

Biochemical hypotheses are those that distinguish personality groups based on body shape (somatotype). The German psychiatrist Ernst Kretschmer developed that morphological theory. He wrote in his book Physique and Character, first published in 1921, that a frail, rather weak (asthenic) bodybuilding as well as a muscular (athletic) physique were frequently characteristic of schizophrenic patients among his patients, while a short, rotund (pyknic) building was often found among manic-depressant patients. Kretschmer expanded his observations and conclusions in a theory of bodybuilding and personality in all men, and wrote that slender and delicate muscles was correlated with introversion, while those with rounded heavier and shorter bodies appear to be cyclothymic — that is, moody but often extroverted and jovial.

Personality research also began to consider the broader social context in which a person lived during the 1930's. Margaret Mead, the American anthropologist, researched patterns of collaboration and competition in 13 primitive societies and was able to document wide variations in those behaviors in different cultures. In her book Gender and Temperament in Three Primitive Societies (1935), she demonstrated that it is not necessarily through aggressiveness that masculinity is expressed and that femininity is not necessarily expressed through passivity and consent. Such observed differences in personality characteristics raised questions about the relative functions of genetics, learning, and cultural pressures.

Theory by Sigmund Freud

Perhaps the most influential integrative personality theory is that of psychoanalysis, widely promulgated by the Austrian neurologist Sigmund Freud during the first four decades of the 20th century. Although its origins were focused on psychopathology research, psychoanalysis became a more general view on the healthy development and functioning of the personality. The research field started with case studies of so-called neurotic cases, which included hysteria, obsessive-compulsive disorders, and phobic conditions. Freud reasoned that the previous experience of seduction imparted its pathogenic force to the later one. Freud initially embraced many of the encounters recorded as real seductions by his young, outstanding patients. He later came to believe that many of the myths, though not all, were hallucinations. Built on this assumption, Freud proposed a hypothesis suggesting that such encounters and other stressful or upsetting occurrences mold personality. He postulated that the sexual trauma hallucinations were manifestations of a sex drive. Instead, in Freud's therapeutic approach, the quest for actual sexual abuse was replaced by an examination of how the sexual inclinations of people, which were already present in childhood, were reflected in behavior. Neurosis and personality, in general, came to be seen as the product of the tension between sexual desires and protection against them, the conflict is embedded in the development of early childhood.

Carl Jung Theory

Archetype was a concept introduced by the Swiss psychiatrist Carl Jung who believed that patterns were models of persons, behaviors, or personalities. He suggested that patterns were inborn tendencies that play a role in influencing human behavior. Jung believed that the human psyche consisted of three components: the ego, the personal unconscious, and the collective unconscious.1 According to Jung, the ego reflects the conscious mind. In contrast, the personal unconscious includes memories, including those suppressed. The collective unconscious is a unique aspect in which Jung assumed this psyche element acted as a form of psychological inheritance. This included all the knowledge and the interactions that we share as a group. The archetypes in Jungian psychology reflect universal patterns and images which form part of the collective unconscious. Jung claimed we inherited these archetypes much the way we inherited automatic behavioral patterns.

4.2 Myer's Brigg 16 Personality Types

Have you ever heard anyone describe himself as an INTJ or an ESTP, and wondered what those enigmatic letters could mean? What those people refer to is their type of personality based on the Myers-Briggs Type Indicator (MBTI). The Myers-Briggs Personality Type Indicator is a self-report checklist designed to identify the essence, abilities, and desires of a person's personality. Isabel Myers and her mother, Katherine Briggs, created the questionnaire based on their experience with the theory of personality types developed by Carl Jung. Both Isabel Myers and her mother, Katherine, we're fascinated by Jung's theory of psychological types and acknowledged that the method could have applications in the real world. During the Second World War, Myers and Briggs began researching and developing an instrument that could be used to help understand differences between individuals. In encouraging people to understand themselves, Myers and Briggs claimed they could help people choose jobs best suited to their styles of personality and lead safer, happier lives. During the 1940s, Myers developed the first pen-and-pencil version of the product, and the two women started testing the measurement on friends and family. Over the next two decades, they continued to develop the instrument in full.

Extraversion (E) – Introversion (I)

Through his theory of personality types, Jung first introduced the dichotomy of extraversion-introversion as a way of describing how people respond and interact with the world around them. Though most people are familiar with these words, the way they are used here is very different from their everyday use.

Extraverts (also often called extroverts) are "outward-turning" and prefer to be action-oriented, enjoy social contact more often, and feel energized after spending time with others. Introverts are "inward-turning" and tend to be thinking-oriented, enjoy deep and meaningful social experiences, and feel recharged after spending time alone. To some extent, we all exhibit extraversion and introversion, but most of us seem to have a preference more for one or the other.

Sensing (S) – Intuition (I)

This scale involves looking at how people collect information from the world around them. As with extraversion and introversion, depending on the situation, all people spend some time sensing and intuiting. People tend to predominate in one region or the other, according to the MBTI. People who prefer sensing manage to pay more attention to the truth, particularly to what they can learn from their senses. We tend to focus on facts and details and enjoy being hands-on. Those who favor intuition pay more attention to such things as patterns and impressions. They enjoy thinking about possibilities, imagining the future, and ideas in abstract.

Thinking (T) – Feeling (F)

This scale focuses on how people make decisions based on the information they obtain from the functions of their sensing or intuition. People who prefer to think put more emphasis on the truth and objective data. When making a decision, they tend to be clear, rational, and impersonal. Before concluding, those who prefer feeling are more likely to consider people and emotions.

Judging (J) – Perceiving (P)

The final scale is how people tend to deal with the world outside. Those who lean to judge prefer order and to make firm decisions. Individuals leaning toward perception are more accessible, more versatile, and more adaptable. Those two patterns interact with those of the other scales. Also, both people spend some extroverted time, at least. The level of judging-perceiving helps to explain whether you are extroverted when taking new knowledge (sensing and intuiting) or when making decisions (thinking and feeling).

The following are the 16 types described, derived from these basic types.

The Inspector-ISTJ Personality

ISTJs are daunting at first sight. They seem serious, formal, and fitting. They also love rituals and old-school ideas that promote patience, hard work, respect, and responsibility for society and culture. They are relaxed, silent, upright, and calm. The combination of I, S, T, and J, a form of personality that is often misunderstood, results in those characteristics.

The Counselor–INFJ Personality

INFJs are visionaries and idealists who ooze brilliant ideas and creative imagination. They have a different, and usually more straightforward, way of looking at the world. We have a substance and complexity in their way of thinking; we never take anything at surface level or embrace things the way they are. Often others may view them as strange or humorous due to their different outlook on life.

The Mastermind-INTJ Type

As introverts, INTJs are quiet, reserved, and happy to be alone. They are generally self-sufficient and would prefer to work alone rather than in a group. Socializing consumes the vitality of an introvert, which necessitates recharging. INTJ's are interested in theories and ideas. You are always curious as you experience the universe why things happen the way they do. We excel in planning and strategic growth and don't like confusion.

The ENFJ – Giver

ENFJ Personality is people-focused people. They are extroverted, idealistic, optimistic, open-minded, extremely conscientious, and ethical and generally know how to communicate with others regardless of their background or personality. They rely primarily on intuition and emotions and tend to live in their imagination rather than the real world. Rather than concentrating on living in the "present" and what's happening at the moment, ENFJs tend to focus on the hypothetical and what might happen in the future.

ISTPs – Enigmatic Type

They are enigmatic people who are generally entirely rational and logical, but also quite spontaneous and enthusiastic. These personality traits are less easily recognizable than those of other groups, and these responses cannot always be expected by even people who know them well. Deep down, ISTPs are wild, unpredictable personalities but, often very effectively, they mask those characteristics from the outside world.

The traditional extroverts are the Provider-ESFJ Personality

ESFJs. They are social butterflies, and they usually end up making them famous through their need to communicate with others and make people happy. The ESFJ generally appears to be the high school and college cheerleader or sports hero. They continue to revel in the spotlight later in life and are focused primarily on organizing social events for their families, friends, and communities. ESFJ is a common type of personality and one that many people like.

The idealists – INFP Type

INFPs have the temperament, like most introverts, are quiet and reserved. They tend not to speak of themselves, particularly in the first-person experience. We like to spend time alone in peaceful environments where they can make sense of what's going on around them. We love to interpret signs and symbols and see them as metaphors that have a deeper meaning to life. Within their imagination and daydreams, they are lost, still trapped in the depths of their minds, visions, and ideas.

The Performer–ESFP Personality

ESFPs have a personality Extraverted, Observant, Feeling and Perceiving, and are commonly viewed as Entertainers. Born to stand before others and grab stage, ESFPs enjoy the spotlight. ESFPs are conscientious seekers who love to learn and to share with others what they know. ESFPs are "men," with excellent interpersonal skills. They are friendly and energetic, and love being the focus of attention. They are dry, compassionate, polite, supportive, and concerned for the well-being of others.

The Champion–ENFP Type

ENFPs have a type of Extraverted, Intuitive, Thinking, and Perceiving. This type of personality is highly individualistic, and Champions strive to create their strategies, appearances, acts, behaviors and ideas— they don't like people who cut cookies and hate being forced to live inside a box. When it comes to themselves and others, they want to be around other people and have an excellent intuitive temperament. Most of the time, they work from their emotions and are incredibly perceptive and considerate.

The Doer-ESTP Type

ESTPs have a type of Extraverted, Sensing, Conscious, and Perceptive. The need for social interaction, feelings, and emotions, rational processes, and reasoning, along with a need for independence, rules ESTPs. Theory and abstracts do not hold an interest in ESTP for long. Instead of sitting idle or making contingency plans, ESTPs jump before they look, correcting their mistakes as they go.

The Manager–ESTJ

They are coordinated, trustworthy, committed, dignified, traditional, and are firm believers in doing what they believe is right and socially acceptable. Though the roads to "good" and "right" are daunting, they are happy to take their place as pack leaders. We represent the epitome of good citizenship. People look for advice and support from ESTJs, and ESTJs are always pleased to be asked for help.

The Commander–ENTJ Personality

An ENTJ's dominant way of living is based on external issues, and all problems are rationally and logically dealt with. A secondary operating mode is internal, in which intuition and logic take effect. ENTJs are naturally born leaders among the 16 forms of personality and like to be in control. We live in a world of possibility and often see difficulties and barriers as high chances of moving themselves forward. We seem to have a natural gift for leadership, decision making, and quickly but carefully considering choices and ideas. We are men who "take charge" and don't like sitting still.

The Thinker-INTP Type

INTPs are well known for their insightful ideas and endless reasoning, which makes sense as they are arguably the most logical thinking of all forms of type. We love patterns, have a keen eye to pick up on inconsistencies, and an excellent ability to read people, making lying to an INTP a lousy idea. Individuals of this type of personality are not interested in practical, day-to-day tasks and maintenance, but when they find an atmosphere where their creative creativity and ability can be displayed, there is no time limit, and INTPs can spend their energies on creating an informative and objective solution.

The ISFJ's Nurturer

ISFJ Personality is philanthropists and is always willing to give back and repay generosity with even greater kindness. The people and things that they believe in will be upheld with enthusiasm and unselfishness and support. The ISFJs are dry and courteous. We respect peace and cooperation, and will, therefore, be very sensitive to the feelings of other people. People value the ISFJ for their empathy and understanding, as well as their ability to make the best out of others.

The Visionary-ENTP Personality

Those with the personality of the ENTP are some of the world's rarest, which is entirely understandable. They do not like small talk, although they are extroverts and may not excel in many social situations, especially those involving people who are too different from the ENTP. ENTPs are knowledgeable and must be continuously mentally stimulated with information. We have the ability to debate hypotheses and evidence in depth. Their approach to facts and claims is logical, rational, and objective.

The Composer – ISFP

ISFP Personality is introverted that does not seem to be introverts. It is because even though at first they have difficulty communicating with other people, they gradually become moist, open, and polite. They're fun to be with and very casual, making them the ideal friend to tag along in any activity, whether scheduled or unplanned. ISFPs want to live their lives to the fullest and enjoy the moment, so they are always on their way to exploring new things and discovering new experiences. We find wisdom in practice, so they see more interest in meeting new people than do other introverts.

4.3 Big Five Personality Test

The attributes of the Big Five are transparency, conscientiousness, extraversion, congeniality, and neuroticism. The definition of personality traits of the "Big Five" is taken from psychology and includes five broad domains that characterize personality. These five personality traits are used to understand personality relationships with different behaviors. It is believed that these five variables reflect the underlying structure behind all character traits. Various different researchers have identified and listed these five factors over multiple periods of study. However, the Big Five personality traits are not nearly as strong predictors and explaining actual behavior as are the more numerous lower-level, specific characteristics, as a result of their broad definitions.

The Five Traits

The Five traits are:
- Openness-Openness to experience defines a person's degree of intellectual curiosity, imagination, and novelty, and variety choice. There is still some controversy over how to perceive the aspect, also called intelligence.
- Conscientiousness – Awareness is a propensity to display self-discipline, behave dutifully, and strive for achievement. Awareness also applies to plan, preparation, and efficiency.
- Extraversion–Extraversion is a concept of strength, positive emotions, assertiveness, sociability, talking ability, and a propensity to seek pleasure in others' company.
- Agreeability–Agreeability is a propensity to be more accommodating and friendly towards others than cynical and antagonistic towards others.
- Neuroticism is a concept of vulnerability to negative emotions such as frustration, anxiety, depression, or weakness. Neuroticism also refers to the emotional stability and impulse control level of a person and is sometimes referred to as emotional stability.

Chapter 5: Emotional Intelligence

The ability to understand, use and control your own emotions in constructive ways to relieve tension, communicate effectively, empathize with others, overcome challenges and defuse conflict is emotional intelligence (otherwise known as the emotional quotient or EQ). Emotional intelligence helps you build stronger relationships, be successful in school and work, and achieve your career and personal goals. It can also help you communicate with your emotions, turn purpose into action, and make informed decisions about what matters most to you.

5.1 Understanding Emotional Intelligence

A lot of us know about the IQ (Intelligence Quotient). This generates a score from a series of tests designed to measure intellectual intelligence. Higher IQs reflect more exceptional cognitive abilities or the ability to understand and know. People with higher IQs are more likely to do academically well without having to spend the same amount of mental energy as those with lower IQ scores. Therefore a reasonable assumption is that people with higher IQs will be more productive at work and throughout their lives. Academic aptitude (IQ) has no relation to how people understand and cope with their emotions and other people's emotions (EI). That makes perfect sense: we've all met brilliant people who nevertheless had no idea how to deal with men and the other way around. Many people have high IQs and low emotional intelligence and vice versa, whereas some people do not score highly on both. Emotional intelligence is one part of the human psyche that we can develop and improve by learning new skills and practicing them. IQ and personality are more permanent metrics and are likely to remain relatively stable throughout your life (although you can improve the ability to complete IQ tests successfully).

For most people, emotional intelligence (EI) is more critical to attaining success in their lives and careers than one's intellect (IQ). As individuals, our success and the success of the profession today depend on our ability to read and respond appropriately to the signals of other people. Each of us, therefore, needs to develop the mature emotional intelligence skills required to understand better, empathize, and negotiate with others— especially as the world has become more global. Otherwise, success in our lives and careers will fail us. Your EI is the extent of your ability to understand other people, what motivates them, and how to work with them in collaboration, "says Howard Gardner, the prominent theorist at Harvard.

Empathy is typically associated with EI since it relates to an individual sharing their personal experiences with others. There are, however, several models for measuring levels of (empathy) EI. There are several EI models currently available. The original Goleman model can now be called a hybrid model incorporating what has since been modeled separately as EI capacity and EI characteristics. Goleman described EI as the array of skills and traits that drive success in leadership. In 2001 Konstantinos V. Petrides created the trait model. It "comprises behavioral patterns and self-perceived capacity, and is assessed by self-reporting." The skill model, founded in 2004 by Peter Salovey and John Mayer, focuses on the capacity of the person to process emotional information and use it for managing the social environment. Studies have shown that people with high EI have greater mental wellbeing, job performance, and leadership skills. However, no causal associations have been confirmed, and such results are likely to be due to general intelligence and specific personality characteristics rather than emotional intelligence as a construct. Goleman, for example, suggested that EI accounted for 67 percent of the abilities deemed necessary for superior leadership success, and imported twice as much as technical expertise or IQ. Other research finds that the impact of EI markers on leadership and managerial efficiency is non-significant when adjusted for skill and temperament. That general intelligence is very carefully related to administration. In the past decade, EI indicators and methods of achieving it have become more commonly sought by individuals who aspire to become more effective leaders. Furthermore, experiments have started to provide evidence that will help describe the emotional intelligence neural mechanisms.

Examples of Emotional Intelligence with Explanation

- Comprehending your feelings: How would you like to learn how to manage your feelings before you understand them? Understating your emotions is the first step to becoming emotionally aware.
- Before taking action, reason about the emotion: Emotional decisions usually lead to wrong actions. For example, being angry could inspire you to do something you later regret. You will become more emotionally intelligent by reasoning before you act.
- Putting yourself in other people's shoes: emotional intelligence also means putting yourself in others ' shoes so you can find an excuse for their behavior. For instance, if you were a manager and one employee did not work

hard. It would be emotionally intelligent to conclude explicitly that he is lazy or unwilling to work, but instead, you should investigate his case more closely to see if there are other factors behind it. You may find he is scared of making mistakes, or you may find he lacks self-confidence in his abilities.

Lack of emotional intelligence can lead to depression and continually feeling bad. Within my novel, the definitive guide to overcoming depression, I explained how depression could not be healed unless it is treated with the root cause that caused it. You might be coping with the wrong problems without emotional intelligence without paying attention to the real ones that are the reason behind your depression.

Example

Two people at work had a fight with their boss. One of them was wise in terms of feeling, and the other was not. The first, who was not emotionally intelligent, started shouting at his children on returning to their homes. This guy acted based on his feelings, without emotionally creative thinking about them. When the second person came home and found the kids were noisy he just said to himself, "Well, why should I shout at the kids; they're not the ones to blame for my feelings, they always make that loud noise while playing. The main reason I feel bad is because of my boss. "That person recognized his emotions, thought of them, then acted emotionally smart.

5.2 Types of Emotional Intelligence

Have you ever known people who always seem to be calm, capable of gracefully coping with even the most awkward social circumstances, and who always seem to make others feel comfortable? There is a reasonably high probability that those people would possess what psychologists call emotional intelligence. The ability to understand and control feelings requires emotional intelligence. Experts agree that such data plays a vital role in the performance, and some have indicated that emotional information could be even more important than IQ. Research has suggested, in any case, that emotional intelligence is associated with everything from decision making to academic achievement. You will learn to be emotionally autonomous and acquire the qualities that enable you to have emotional intelligence by listening to core emotions, embracing them, and understanding how they affect your decisions and actions. Being able to relate attitudes and emotional intelligence issues to success in the workplace is an enormous asset in building an outstanding team. One of the most common factors contributing to issues relating to retention is communication deficits that generate disengagement and doubt. So what does it take to become emotionally smart? Psychologist and best-selling author, Daniel Goleman has indicated that emotional intelligence has five critical components to it. Take a look at these five variables and see if there might be something you can do in each area to improve your skills.

Self-Awareness

Self-awareness is a critical part of emotional intelligence or the ability to recognize and appreciate one's own emotions. And, beyond just knowing your feelings, you are aware of the effect of other people's actions, moods, and emotions. To order to become self-aware, you need to be able to monitor your feelings, recognize different emotional responses, and then interpret each particular emotion correctly. Self-conscious individuals often understand the connection between the things that they experience and the way they act. Some individuals are also able to recognize their strengths and limitations, are open to new information and experiences, and benefit from interactions with others. Goleman suggests that people who have this knowledge of themselves have a good sense of humor, are sure of themselves and their abilities, and are conscious of how others view them.

Self-Regulation

Besides being aware of your own emotions and their effect on others, emotional intelligence demands that you be able to regulate and manipulate your emotions. This doesn't mean lock-down emotions and suppressing your real feelings — it just says waiting for the right time, place, and avenue to share your opinions. Self-regulation is about giving proper voice to your tastes. Those who can regulate themselves tend to be versatile and respond well to change. We are also good at conflict management and at diffusing awkward or complicated circumstances. Goleman also suggests high sensitivity among those with strong self-regulation skills. We think about how we affect other people and take responsibility for their actions.

Social Skills

Another critical aspect of emotional intelligence is being able to interact well with others. Pure emotional awareness requires more than just knowing one's own emotions and other people's feelings-you also need to be able to put this insight into your daily interactions and communications. Managers benefit from being able to build relationships and ties with employees in professional settings. In contrast, employees may benefit from being able to develop a strong relationship with leaders and co-workers. Many critical social skills include active listening, oral communication skills, nonverbal communication skills, leadership, and persuasiveness.

Empathy

Empathy is critical to emotional intelligence or the ability to understand how others feel. But this means more than just being able to recognize other people's emotional states. It also includes the responses based on that information to others. For example, when you know someone is feeling sad or helpless, it will probably influence how you react to that person. You could handle them with extra care and concern, or you could make an effort to breathe in their spirits. Feeling empathetic often helps people to understand the dynamics of power that often affect social relationships, especially in workplace environments. Those who are knowledgeable in this area can sense who has control in different relationships, understand how these forces affect feelings and actions, and accurately interpret different situations that rely on such dynamics of power.

Motivation

Emotional intelligence also plays a crucial role in intrinsic motivation. Emotionally intelligent people are driven by things beyond mere external rewards such as fame, wealth, acknowledgment, and acclamation. They are passionate about meeting their own inner needs and goals. We are looking for things that contribute to intrinsic rewards, knowledge flowing from being entirely in touch with an operation, and seek peak experiences. Those who have expertise in this field tend to be action-oriented. They set goals, have a high need for accomplishment, and always find ways to do better. They also seem to be very dedicated, and they are good at taking the initiative when they face a challenge.

5.3 Importance of Emotional Intelligence

Will you accept the feelings you feel? Could you control those sensations without letting them overwhelm you? Can you get yourself inspired to get jobs done? Can you think of other people's emotions, and respond effectively? If you answered yes to these questions, you've probably developed some or all of the skills that form the foundation of emotional intelligence. Emotional intelligence (EI) creates the juncture at which cognition and emotion meet; it enhances our capacity for endurance, inspiration, empathy, reasoning, stress management, communication, and our ability to read and handle a multitude of social situations and conflicts. EI matters and, if practiced, offers one the opportunity to live a fuller and happier life.

The word ' Emotional Intelligence,' first coined by psychologists Mayer and Salovey (1990), refers to one's ability to accurately and effectively interpret, process, and control emotional information, both within oneself and in others, and to use this knowledge to direct one's thoughts and actions and to influence others'. Emotional intelligence may lead us on the road to a fulfilled and happy life by providing a structure for applying intelligence principles to emotional responses, and recognizing that these responses may be logically consistent or inconsistent with particular passionate beliefs. As the workplace evolves, so does the research body supporting that individuals (from interns to managers) with higher EI are better equipped to work cohesively within teams, deal more effectively with change and manage stress–thus enabling them to pursue business goals more efficiently. Therefore, EI, unlike its relatively fixed counterpart, IQ, is instead a complicated component of one's personality and contains behavioral traits that can produce significant benefits when worked on, ranging from personal happiness and wellbeing to elevated professional success.

Emotional intelligence has been shown to play a meaningful role in academic success, mental and physical health, as well as professional achievement; Bar-On's results (1997) suggest that people with higher EI performed better in life than those with lower EI. EI's importance should not be overlooked; the ability to understand and manage your emotions is the first step towards realizing your true potential. How can we make meaningful progress if we don't recognize and acknowledge the point we start from? A destination will be useless when checking directions on your sat-nav unless we know the sources. Whether it's communicating with others and enhancing interpersonal communication, achieving workplace or social relationships success, coping with stress and increasing motivation, or developing decision-making skills–emotional intelligence plays a central role in achieving success both in personal and professional life.

Emotional Intelligence and Decision-Making

Emotional intelligence is closely related to personal and professional growth. It affects more than how we handle our actions and navigate social dynamics, and how we make decisions. Getting a clear view of the emotions we experience and why we feel them can have a significant impact on our decision-making skills. If we are unable to look objectively at our feelings, how can we avoid making irrational decisions based on them? Superior emotional intelligence is an essential element in the prevention of emotionally biased decision-making, while lower EI can cause anxiety and lead to poor decision-making. It is not about completely removing emotions from the decision-making process, but rather about recognizing the feelings that are unrelated to the problem and not allowing them to be influential to the outcome. Negative emotions can impair organizational problem-solving and decision-making, as well as personal circumstances. The ability to recognize feelings that are superfluous in forming a rational decision, and the ability to effectively suppress those emotions, negating their impact on the outcome, has distinct advantages for decision-making processes.

Through a series of questions and observations with a focus on improving understanding of EI and using EI skills to improve the decision-making process, Hess & Bacigalupo (2011) found that organizations and individuals benefited from the practical application of EI in decision-making scenarios. The observations suggest that EI training is an effective strategy to implement when developing decision-making skills and assists in understanding the potential consequences of bad decision-making. Considering the emotional causes and consequences allows an individual to control both the feeling and make an objective decision. Imagine you have a disagreement with your partner and go to work angry and stressed out a little bit, later that day you reject a colleague's proposal without really paying attention to what they suggest–you're just not in the mood. The decision-making process can be counterproductive to this form of emotional intervention; those with more defined EI can recognize and handle this kind of emotional involvement and prevent emotionally driven decisions.

5.4 Values and Benefits of Emotional Intelligence

The values and benefits of emotional intelligence in terms of both personal and professional success are enormous. In many vocations, it is a core competency, will help progression to be an academic and professional achievement, strengthen relationships, and develop communication skills, the list continues. Bar-On (1997) goes so far as to suggest that people with higher EI tend to perform better in life overall, regardless of IQ, than those with lower EI. There has been much debate about the benefits of teaching EI in classrooms, with a focus on the premise that emotionally smart kids grow up to become emotionally intelligent adults. EI skills become a critical prerequisite in extensive or intensive' emotional work ' fields such as nursing, social work, the service industry, and management roles. High EI improves people's physical and psychological health and promotes academic and business performance (Bar-On & Parker, 2000). Emotional intelligence is part and parcel of the formation and development of meaningful human relationships. Schutte et al. (2001) found that essential linkages between high EI and more productive interpersonal relationships existed over a series of studies. Some participants who displayed higher levels of EI also demonstrated a greater propensity to take empathic perspectives, to collaborate with others, to develop affectionate and more rewarding relationships, and to generally increase social skills.

It is important to note that self-awareness–the ability to manage emotions and stress–and the ability to solve personal, as well as interpersonal issues, are also directly linked to physical health. Chronic stress can cause adverse effects that accompany it, such as frustration, depression, and anxiety may precipitate the development and progression of hypertension, heart problems, and diabetes. It may increase susceptibility to viruses and infections; may delay healing of wounds and injuries; and may intensify conditions such as arthritis and atherosclerosis (Bar-On, 2006; Black & Garbutt, 2002). The value of EI is immense; cultivating emotional intelligence facilitates several positive traits, ranging from resilience to communication, encouragement to stress reduction, all of which can be seen as conducive to achieving excellent mental, physical, and occupational health and performance.

Resilience and Emotional Intelligence

Emotional intelligence is undoubtedly a valuable tool to use in the face of adversity; it has the ability to improve not only leadership skills and effectiveness of teamwork but also personal resiliency. Focusing on the effect of EI on one's resilience, that is, one's ability to cope with stressful conditions, research suggests that those with higher levels of emotional intelligence are less likely to succumb to stressors ' negative impacts.

In the sense of a leadership role, increased responsibility could be expected to correlate with elevated potential stressors, emphasizing the importance of good EI for those in leadership or management positions. An inquiry into the relationship between emotional intelligence and the stress cycle found that participants exhibiting higher levels of EI were less likely to be adversely affected by stressors. Participants completed an EI skill-based test before determining the subjectively perceived level of threat presented by two stressors, then self-reported their emotional response to said stressors, and were also subjected to physiological stress-response tests to determine their response.

In short, those with higher levels of emotional intelligence were also more resilient and less likely to' burnout' or succumb to depression. Such results are based on previous research that found EI ratings to have been positively correlated with psychological wellbeing while being negatively associated with depression and burnout. The study highlighted the possible ability to reduce one's vulnerability to depression through strategies to improve EI (Lin, Liebert, Tran, Lau, & Salles 2016) despite the dynamic nature of EI. Ironically, EI is strongly correlated with individual success and efficiency, with evidence suggesting a significant connection between one's resilience and one's desire to attain (Magnano, Craparo & Paolillo, 2016). Besides, resistance is proposed to play a mediating function between EI and self-motivated achievement. In other words, emotional intelligence is a precondition for resilience, and resilience can lead to increased motivation. Resistance has an underlying aspect of perseverance, which motivates resilience against challenges (Luthans, Avey & Avolio, 2010).

5.5 Link between Emotional Intelligence and Job Performance

The growing awareness of emotional intelligence in management-focused literature and leadership training shows that not only the link between emotional intelligence and job performance exists, but it also has importance in various fields.

The workplace represents a different social community, detached from our personal lives, in which there is a growing appreciation that higher EI allows a person to understand themselves and others better, to communicate more effectively, and to cope with the challenges. The use and growth of emotional intelligence in the workplace will significantly improve individuals ' personal and social abilities within that workplace. EI is about controlling emotions to boost job performance and, in effect, help people stay calm and think critically so that a good relationship can be formed and goals accomplished. There is an undeniable link between EI and how senior managers handle their staff-managers with higher emotional intelligence have the tools at their disposal not only to manage stress but also to identify and resolve the tension in others.

When we think of emotional intelligence in terms of stress management and relationship building, the connection between emotional intelligence skills and job performance is evident, with stress management having a positive impact on work engagement and satisfaction. It is also important to note that EI not only exists at management level, but workers with advanced emotional intelligence skills lower the company hierarchy also have the desire and ability to establish and maintain high-quality organizational relationships (Lopes, Salovey, & Straus, 2003). Furthermore, high-EI individuals are better equipped to handle conflict efficiently and, besides, maintain relationships within the workplace relative to those with low to moderate EI rates.

Organizations increasingly realize the importance of workers who possess the skills to manage change and respond accordingly. EI is an essential factor in the performance of workers at both the individual and group levels; nevertheless, as a person moves up a hierarchy of the organization, the positive impact of emotional intelligence on dealing with circumstances and effectively completing tasks increases (Moghadam, Tehrani & Amin, 2011).

Emotional Intelligence and Motivation

Emotional intelligence counts for motivation and achievement problems for motivation. Whether concerning work, personal ambitions, or wellbeing, the emotionally intelligent individual recognizes the deeper meaning of their expectations and the skills required for self-motivation to achieve them. Goleman (1995) described four driving elements: our desire to change, our dedication to the goals we set for ourselves, our willingness to act on opportunities presented to us, and our resilience. Magnano et al. (2016) suggest that motivation is the underlying psychological process that we use to motivate ourselves into action to achieve the desired result. Whether it is picking up the remote to change the television channel or devoting hundreds of hours to deliver a project, we would be unable to act without motivation.

Motivation enhances, energizes, and drives actions and performance. Intrinsic motivation, that is, inspiration from within, encourages us to achieve our full potential. An Emotionally Intelligent person has not only the skills for self-motivation but also the skills needed to inspire others, a valuable talent to have in management positions in particular. Although self-motivation is central to achieving one's goals, the motivation of workers can also be influenced by emotionally intelligent business leaders. The ability to recognize the feelings and, in turn, other people's concerns is an important skill to have at the fingertips in terms of understanding the most effective ways of inspiring teams and people. In a recent study, the first-year medical graduates ' EI rates are positively linked to self-motivation to study medicine and satisfaction with choosing medicine (Edussuriya, Marambe, Tennakoon, Rathnayake, Premaratne, Ubhayasiri, & Wickramasinghe, 2018). A study of senior managers with high IE employed in organizations in the public sector found that IE increases positive work attitudes, altruistic behavior, and work outcomes. Unsurprisingly, it seems that happy employees are motivated employees. For example, the ability to better cope with stress and anxiety is also a valuable motivational EI resource–if one can identify the feelings that may affect motivation negatively, they can be handled and controlled effectively (Carmeli, 2003).

Emotional Intelligence and Success

Just like happiness, ask someone to define success, and you're likely to get more than one response. Does it make your career successful? Your instinct? How much money hast thou? Feel happiness and contentment? That can be anything depending on who you ask. What is clear is that emotional intelligence can play a vital role in achieving it no matter what your definition of success is. It's not always the smartest people who meet the most significant success, as discussed. IQ alone is not enough to make living excellence. You may be the most intelligent person in the room, but if you don't have an EI, do you have the ability to calm down negative thoughts or the ability to manage stress? Goleman (1995) identified EI as powerful and, at times, more powerful than IQ in predicting lifetime success. It is the Emotional Intelligence that helps you achieve your goals and achieve higher performance rates. Developing EI will significantly influence our progress by leading to improved integrity, motivation, and collaboration (Strickland, 2000).

In the workplace, managers who consistently outperform their peers have not only technical knowledge and experience, but more importantly, they use EI-related strategies to manage conflicts, reduce stress, and thus improve their success. There is growing evidence that the range of skills that comprise what is now commonly referred to as' emotional intelligence' plays a crucial role in determining performance–both in one's personal life and in the workplace–with real-life implications extending to parenting, relationships, companies, medical professionals, service workers and so much more.

Emotional intelligence helps one to control emotions in anxiety-provoking circumstances such as taking tests at school or university and also has positive associations with performance in personal relations and social functioning. Achievement within social relationships can be gained by using EI competencies to discover others' emotional states, adopt others' perspectives, enhance communication, and regulate behavior.

Chapter 6: Understanding Psychology

Psychology is a broad field covering the study of human thought, behavior, development, personality, emotion, motivation, and more. Gaining a more productive and more in-depth understanding of psychology will help people gain insights into their behavior and a better understanding of others as well.

It is safe to say, when it comes to human behavior, that there are many ways to formulate and evaluate it. The same goes for psychological awareness. Let's not forget that psychology is the course that looks for an explanation of the mental processes and the expression of human behavior. That being said, it's hard not to ask yourself how some unanimity can be reached in making sense of human actions when there are so many viewpoints from which to view it.

When it comes to studying how people think, feel, and act, psychologists, use different approaches. Whatever method, the research object is invariable, and the results are typically not far from each other. We will be throwing out some hints in this chapter that will make learning psychology a little easier. Several scholars have decided to focus on one specific school of thought. Others, on the other hand, opt for a more diverse approach that combines different viewpoints. Essentially, by definition, not one view is better than another; each of them underlines various aspects of human nature, and it is up to you to concentrate on when trying to understand psychology. From a psychological point of view, an approach is a viewpoint that suggests some conclusions regarding human behavior, which are distinct from other theories that other schools tackle. There may be several different theories within the same branch, but when they come under the same school, they all share similar foundations.

The behavioral approach

Behaviorism is different from most other methods since their environment typically influences humans (as well as animals) according to it. We're, in essence, the product of what we've observed in terms of triggers, reinforces, and connections for behaviorism. Therefore behaviorism investigates how observed behavior (response) is influenced by environmental factors (stimuli).
The behavioral theory suggests two primary mechanisms by which people learn from their environment: classical conditioning and conditioning of operations. We can see the classical conditioning expressed in the experiments of Ivan Pavlov and the B.F. operant. Skinner. According to the behavioral approach, measurable behavior should only be observed, because it is the only one that can be assessed. Behaviorism, in turn, rejects the idea that individuals have free will. As we said above, it assumes that the world of the person dictates all of their approaches.

The cognitive approach

The cognitive approach surrounds the idea that we have to learn what runs through their minds if we want to know what makes people do certain things. This method of studying psychology is thus based on the study of mental processes. In other terms, the psychologist's research thought from a cognitive perspective, meaning the spiritual act or mechanism through which people acquire information. Besides, the cognitive approach also deals with mental functions, including memory, vision, and focus. Cognitivist takes the view that humans in the way they process information are close to computers.

The Biological Approach

The biological approach explains actions by the underlying genomics of the organism. Above all, it explores how genes affect the activities of humans. This is a very different way of understanding psychology as it assumes specific patterns are inherited and have an adaptive function. The biological approach is focused on the interpersonal interaction with the supporting brain structures. So it searches for the causes of actions in gene expression, brain, nervous system, and endocrine systems. In other words, it seeks to study how all of these systems interact. Therefore, psych biologists research how actions, emotions, and thoughts connect the human body. In this way, it tries to know how the mind and body work together to create ideas, memories, and perceptions of the senses.

The Humanistic Approach

The humanistic approach studies a person as an integral, complete entity. Humanistic psychologists not only observe human behavior through the eyes of the observer but through the eyes of the person itself. It underlines the significance of understanding the confluence of the essential spheres of every single person. From this way of understanding psychology, people's actions are thought to be linked to their inner feelings and to the perception they hold of themselves. The humanistic approach focuses on the concept of a person being exceptional and having the freedom to change any time in life. This view suggests we are all in control of our own happiness. Therefore we have an inherent self-realization capacity which pushes our desire to develop our potential.

6.1 How Everyone Reads People

Empathy makes us feel other people's emotions, recognize and understand their feelings, motivations and see things from their perspective. In cognitive science, how we produce empathy remains a subject of intense debate. Now some scientists believe they may have found the origin at last. Necessarily, we just mind readers, they say. The concept was slow to gain acceptance but there is mounting evidence. It's about understanding what other people want to be doing, beyond words. It's about knowing what they think, even if they're saying otherwise. The ability to read people properly can influence your social, family, and work-life significantly. If you understand how another person feels, then you can tailor your message and communication style to ensure that it is handled in the best possible way. It is not that difficult. This may sound cliché, but no special powers are required to know how to read people.

Over the years, cognitive scientists have developed a set of theories to explain how cognition and thinking process progresses. Currently, two of the most famous are "theory theory" and "simulation theory." The idea portrays children as potential social scientists. The idea is that kids gather evidence— in the form of movements and expressions— and use their collective understanding of people to build hypothesis that describe and predict the mental state of the people they come into contact with. Another name for this hypothesis is Vittorio Gallese, a neuroscientist at the University of Parma in Italy and one of the initial pioneers of mirror neurons. He named it the "Vulcan Approach," in honor of Star Trek's protagonist Spock, which fits the race belongs to an alien called the Vulcans, who suppressed their emotions in favor of rationality. Also, Spock couldn't understand the feelings behind human behavior.

Simulation theory states that we are observers of the human mind. We place ourselves in the "thinking shoes" of another human and use our account as a guide for theirs. Gallese argues that we do more than just analyze the actions of the other person when we communicate with someone. He claims we create internal representations within ourselves of their acts, perceptions and feelings, as if we are the ones who are moving, sensing and feeling. Most scientists believe that the neurons in the mirror reflect simulation theory predictions. "Not only do we share with others the way they normally act or perceive emotions and sensations subjectively, but also the neural circuits that activate those same acts, emotions, and sensations: the mirror neuron systems," Gallese told LiveScience.

Nevertheless, Gallese points out that neither principle is mutually exclusive. If the mirror neuron system is flawed or impaired, and our ability to empathize is lost, the theory's observation-and-guess approach may be the only option left. Many psychologists believe this is what happens with autistic people whose mental disorder impedes them from understanding other people's motivations and motives.

The theory is that autistic people's mirror neuron structures are somehow defective or damaged and that the resulting "mind-blindness" prevents them from simulating others' experiences. For autistic individuals, the experience is more experienced than lived, and inaccessible are the emotional undercurrents that rule so much of our human behavior. Through current theorizing, they infer the mental states of others. Still, the result is a list— automatic and impersonal— of actions, movements, and expressions void of motive, intent, or emotion. Many laboratories are now investigating the theory that autistic individuals have a mirror neuron deficiency and can't mimic other people's mental states. One recent experiment by Hugo Theoret and colleagues at the University of Montreal showed that the mirror neurons normally active in non-autistic individuals when observing hand movements are silent in those with autism. You either replicate with mirror neurons, or you're entirely excluded from the mental states of others, "Iacoboni said.

6.2 Our Mind and the way we communicate

Neuroscience (the research that explores how the brain functions) keeps telling us new things about the importance of the prefrontal cortex in our daily lives. Tell yourself: will you say the same personal stuff you tell your family and friends to a stranger, like a treasured memory? Scientists found that patients with severe damage to the prefrontal cortex had said such personal things to strangers, even though afterward, they felt embarrassed. Yet, why didn't the patients know that they were talking to a stranger? Could it be that we need the prefrontal cortex to change our speech? The act of conveying one idea or thought from one person to another. Is it dependent on the person we interact with?

It is no longer just for Spock to reach into someone's brain directly to share thoughts. An international team of researchers tested the Vulcan Mind Meld by designing a device that allows two people to share knowledge through reflection. The researchers tested the system by splitting the users from each other more than 8,000 km (5,000 mi) apart— with one user in France and another in India. We wanted to find out if one could communicate directly between two individuals by reading out one person's brain activity and inserting brain activity into the second person, and by exploiting existing communication channels to do so over great physical distances. By using advanced precision neuro technologies like wireless EEG and robotic TMS, we were able to transmit a thought directly and non-invasively from one human to another, without them speaking or writing. This in itself is an extraordinary step in human communication, but being able to do so over a distance of thousands of miles is a critically important proof-of-principle for brain-to-brain communication progress. We conclude that these studies represent an essential first step in investigating the feasibility of complementing or bypassing conventional communication based on language or motor.

6.3 Unconscious Mind

While we are entirely aware of what is happening in the conscious mind, we have no idea what information the unconscious mind is filled with. The unconscious includes all manner of essential and upsetting content that we need to keep out of consciousness because they are too dangerous to acknowledge fully.

The unconscious mind functions as a store, a' cauldron' of primal desires and urges that are kept at bay and controlled by the preconscious zone. For example, Freud (1915) found that some events and attractions were often too fearful or painful to acknowledge for his patients, and believed that such information was locked away in the unconscious mind. That can happen through the repression process. The unconscious mind includes our biologically based desires (eros and Thanatos) for sex and violent primitive impulses (Freud, 1915). Freud concluded that our primal urges are often intolerable to our moral, aware self. People have developed several mechanisms of defense (such as repression) to prevent understanding what their hidden motivations and emotions are. Freud (1915) underlined the importance of the unconscious mind, and Freudian theory's central premise is that the unconscious mind controls actions to a greater extent than people suspect. Psychoanalysis aims to reveal the use of such mechanisms of defense and thus to make the unconscious conscious. Freud claimed that the unconscious 'forces manifest themselves in a variety of ways, including hallucinations, and tongue slips, now popularly known as' Freudian slips.' Freud (1920) gave an example of such a mistake when a British parliamentarian referred to a colleague with whom he was annoyed as' Honorable Member of Hell' rather than Hull.

6.4 Clusters of Gestures and behavior patterns

Observing body language, individual expressions are rarely noticed. A person often transmits his emotional state through more than one gesture, and that combination of gestures is known as a cluster of gestures. When studying body language, you must include as many movements as possible because that will provide a more detailed and more precise picture of the current emotional state of the individual.

One of the gravest errors a beginner may make in body language is to perceive a single gesture in isolation from other gestures or other circumstances. Scratching the head, for example, can mean a variety of things-dandruff, fleas, sweating, confusion, forgetfulness, or deception, depending on the other movements that occur at the same moment, so we always have to look at gesture clusters for a correct reading. The body language, like any different language, consists of phrases, sentences, and punctuation. Every gesture is like a single word, and the meaning of a word can be many. It is only when you use other words to put the name into a sentence that you can fully understand its meaning. Gestures come in' sentences' and tell the truth inevitably about the thoughts or attitudes of an individual. The' perceptive' person is one who can read the non-verbal sentences and fit them precisely against the verbal sentences of the person.

The behavioral pattern means conduct by one individual in an intimate relationship that is used by fear and intimidation to maintain power and control over the other person in the connection. That would probably be in search of a sense of security, of power, of safety. For this need arises the most common pattern of individual behaviors. The air we breathe is more important to humans. For example, far more people drown because of fear than because they lose all the air, or technically speaking, they intensify the drowning process because they feel they are losing control. The emotional need for a sense of control is so healthy for us humans because it is so profoundly important. Look at any human behavior, and that is the most common pattern you'll find, a need for power and countless ways we humans try to achieve it. I know you've used the word "conduct" in your question, but I'll expand on it by saying that strategies are everywhere. Still, the trend is embedded in the theory (people need to feel they're in control to feel safe, and that's our primary emotional concern), and that's why most common human actions come out of that emotional need.

Chapter 7: Communication Types

Communication means transferring thoughts, knowledge, emotions, and ideas from one person to another via gesture, speech, symbols, signs, and expressions. In any communication cycle, they are sender, receiver, and the channel (medium). Three aspects are the most important and necessary. The sender encodes the messages in any form, such as voice, written, or signs. So they frequently called as encoders. To understand the word, the receiver decodes the sender's address. And they commonly called as decoders. Channel: Every message or information requires a channel or a medium. Example: TV is an audiovisual medium that decodes the audience's electronic signals into an audiovisual. You might think it's easy to master communicative skills. Communication is based on a variety of means, including verbal, body language, written language, and more. The important thing is for you to recognize this and to learn from all the means of communication that are available to you. This way, you can develop valuable communication skills to cope with various circumstances and strengthen your interpersonal relationships.

In-Depth knowledge of the relationship and communication skills process is essential. It is vital to any individual's success at any company. Communication styles change from individual to individual. A person may invoke several channels, modes, or methods to convey a message during the communication process. But, the communication mechanism does not depend solely on the source that produces or relays information. It also depends equally on the method of communication and the way the receiver understands the message. At a given point, the contact starts. The first step to this is knowledge generation. The second step is to put the information or data into a communication medium for the intended audience. During this process, the communication initiator must pay special attention to the nature of the data. The communication skills are to assess their communication efficacy.

We communicate every moment endlessly through different forms, networks, movements, and expressions, all as a natural reflection of our selves. But while our contact is entirely voluntary, it's not always conscious. Often we interact without our conscious knowledge, which leads to inaccurate or even contradictory self-expressions. And the secret to excellent contact lies in there: perception. If we can remain constantly aware of the implicit communication signals we send out at any moment, we can adapt this to represent what we want to communicate. Our communication, then, is no longer accidental; it is entirely incidental. Some moments to communicate? How can it even be? It is not like I open my mouth every minute, "we hear you asking. Yeah, but you see, we're not just talking verbally but also non-verbally, and even informally.

7.1 Verbal Communication

Verbal communication is a kind of oral communication in which the message is transmitted through the words spoken. Here the sender gives words and shares his emotions, observations, ideas, and opinions in the form of interviews, debates, presentations, and conversations. The effectiveness of verbal communication depends on the speaker's tone, speech comprehension, pace, tempo, body language, and the nature of the words used in the conversation. The input is immediate in the case of verbal communication, since there are simultaneous transmission and reception of the message by the sender and receiver, respectively. The sender must keep his speech tone high and audible to all, and the subject matter must be crafted with a view to the target audience. The sender should always cross-check with the recipient to make sure that the message is received exactly as intended. This communication is more prone to errors as the words are sometimes not enough to communicate a person's feelings and emotions. The success of verbal communication depends not only on an individual's speaking ability but also on his listening abilities. The efficacy of the discussion is determined by how well a person listens to the subject matter. Verbal communication occurs in cases of both formal and informal kind.

Verbal communication involves sounds, phrases, speech, and language. Talking is a critical way to communicate and helps to express our feelings through writing. Although the word "verbal communication" seems to be almost self-explanatory as an expression, verbal communication is far more nuanced than just talking. Through definition, verbal communication involves not only oral discussions and interactions but also written messages and even indirect contact that incorporates interface using ICT rather than face-to-face verbal communication. A few types of verbal communication are described below.

Oral Communication

Oral communication is the most evident form of verbal communication, and several examples of oral communication are readily available. All types of verbal communication are speeches, presentations, and announcements, as well as casual conversations between friends. In addition to regular verbal communication, most communication models also include verbal input from the receiver, which may be in the form of questions or remarks, but could be as brief as a simple "Yes" or even an "Uh-huh" non-descript. Although specific examples of verbal, oral communication are virtually unlimited, any interaction involving at least one recipient and at least one transmitter using verbal communication are almost endless.

Written Communication

While it may seem counterintuitive, written communication under the most commonly accepted meanings of the word is considered a form of verbal communication. Defining verbal communication as both written and spoken involves the use of standard communication methods in both types to give meaning: written words and spoken words. A plethora of clearly nonverbal forms of communication can, therefore, be used as examples of verbal communication, including written letters, memos, documents, magazines, journals, and even personal notes. Textbooks, novels, and other literature also serve as examples of verbal communication, as words are used as how a message is conveyed.

Mediated Communication

Although the indirect communication area is a separate branch of the study of communication, it includes examples of both verbal and nonverbal communication. Most of the World Wide Web material consists of either typed text or images, both of which rely heavily on verbal communication to get their messages across. Webcasts and other interactive online media also use verbal communication, as do emails, telnet sessions, and newsgroup messages. Indirect communication does not end with the Internet; television broadcasts use a mixture of verbal and nonverbal communication, and radio broadcasts rely on oral communication. Equally, telephone conversations are active due to the flow of words from a sender to a receiver, enhanced only by variances in sound, inflection, rhythm, and pitch (all of which are also subtle types of verbal communication).

Intrapersonal Communication

This form of communication is extremely private and confined to ourselves. This involves the quiet interactions that we have with ourselves, in which we juggle positions between the sender and the receiver who interpret our thoughts and actions. Once examined, this thinking mechanism can either be verbally communicated to someone or stay confined as thoughts.

Interpersonal communication

This form of communication happens between two persons and is, therefore, a one-on-one interaction. There, the two individuals involved must change their sender and receiver positions so that they can interact more clearly.

Contact by small groups

This type of communication can only take place when more than two people are involved. The number of people here will be small enough to allow each participant to interact with each other and converse with the rest. Types of community contact include press conferences, Board meetings, and team meetings. Unless a particular issue is discussed, the small group discussions can become chaotic and stressful for everyone to interpret. This lag of a complete understanding of knowledge can lead to miscommunication.

Public communication

This type of communication happens when one person is addressing a large gathering of people. Definitions of this type of communication include election campaigns and public speeches. In such instances, there is typically one information sender and several receivers that are sent.

7.2 Non – Verbal Communication

Nonverbal communication refers to gestures, facial expressions, voice tone, eye contact (or lack thereof), body language, posture, and other ways in which people can communicate without the use of words. Your nonverbal communication is almost as critical as your verbal answers when you're interviewing for a job or taking part in a meeting. It can seem protective to have arms crossed. Poor posture can sound unprofessional. A downward gaze or the avoidance of eye contact may distract from being viewed as confident. Employers can judge what you do as well as what you say, and you can make the best impression using your nonverbal communication skills. If your skills aren't top-notch, you should exercise them to make a positive impact on everybody you encounter in and beyond the workplace.

Various channels define this form of communication, and scholars argue that nonverbal communication can convey a more significant meaning than verbal communication. Several researchers say the majority of people prefer nonverbal forms of communication over verbal communication. Ray Birdwhistell concludes that nonverbal communication accounts for 60–70 percent of human interaction, although, according to other researchers, the type of connection is not quantifiable or does not reflect modern human communication, mainly when people rely so much on written means. Charles Darwin began to study nonverbal communication when he observed the interactions between animals and discovered that gestures and movements also conveyed these. Nonverbal contact was first researched and questioned on its importance.

This includes the use of visual signals such as body language (kinesics), distance (proxemics), and physical environments/appearance, speech (paralanguage), and touch (haptics). It may also include the use of time (chronemics) and eye contact as well as observing and listening movements, duration of views, focus patterns, pupil dilation, and blink rate (oculesics).

Just as speech includes nonverbal elements known as paralanguage, including voice quality, pace, pitch, loudness, and speech style, as well as prosodic characteristics such as rhythm, intonation, and tension, so written texts, have nonverbal elements such as handwriting style, spatial word arrangement, or the physical page layout. Much of the nonverbal communication research, however, has concentrated on contact between people, where it can be divided into three main areas: environment conditions where communication takes place, physical communicator characteristics, and communicator actions throughout the interaction. Nonverbal communication involves the encoding and decoding processes that are conscious and unconscious. The method of producing information, such as facial expressions, movements, and postures, is encoding. Encoding information makes use of signals that we would assume are universal. Decoding is the interpretation provided by the encoder of the info from obtained sensations. Decoding information makes use of the experience one may have of some impressions got. The Nonverbal encoding series includes facial expressions, gestures, posture, tone of voice, tactile stimulation such as touch, and movements of the body, such as when someone moves closer to communicate or steps away because of spatial borders. The Decoding process involves the use of sensations experienced in conjunction with previous experience in understanding the meaning of contact with others.

Culture plays a vital role in nonverbal communication, and it is one factor that helps to influence the organization of learning activities. For example, in many Indigenous American Communities, the emphasis is often placed on nonverbal communication, which acts as a valued means of learning for children. In this sense, learning is not based on verbal communication; instead, it is nonverbal communication that serves as a primary means not only of coordinating interpersonal interactions, but also of conveying cultural values, and from a young age, children learn how to engage in this method.

Importance

Nonverbal contact accounts for two-thirds of all interactions, according to some writers. Nonverbal communication may portray a message with the correct body signals or gestures, both locally and. Body signals include physical characteristics, movements, and signs that are conscious and unconscious, and the manipulation of personal space. The wrong message can also be set if a verbal message does not suit the body language communicated.

In everyday situations like attracting a partner or in a business interview, nonverbal communication confirms a first impression: impressions are created on average within the first four seconds of interaction. First experiences or interactions with another person have a substantial impact on the understanding of an individual. When the other person or group receives the message, they concentrate on the whole world around them, meaning that the other person uses all five senses in the interaction: 83% sight, 11% sound, 3% smell, 2% touch, and 1% taste. Many indigenous cultures use nonverbal communication to integrate children into their cultural practices at a young age. In these cultures, children learn by observation and pitching in which nonverbal communication is a crucial aspect of consideration.

Posture

Posture is a nonverbal cue correlated with positioning and that these two are used as sources of information about the qualities, behaviors, and feelings of the person about themselves and other people. There are many different types of the positioning of the body to reflect such postures, including slouching, standing, widening of the thighs, the thrust of the neck, forward shoulders, and crossing of the arm. Individuals' attitude or bodily position conveys several signals, whether good or bad. For example, a study identified around 200 poses related to maladjustment and information withholding. Posture can be used to assess the degree of attention or participation of an individual, the difference of status between the communicators, and the level of affection that a person has for the other communicator, depending on the "openness" of the body. It can also be used effectively as a way for a person to express a desire to increase, restrict, or prevent contact with someone else. Studies investigating the impact of posture on interpersonal relationships suggest that mirror-image congruent attitudes, where the left side of one person is parallel to the right side of the other person, lead to a beneficial views of communicators and positive speech; a person who shows a progressive lean or decreases a reversive lean also signifies positive feeling during communication. Posture can be situation-relative; that is, people will change their stance depending on the situation in which they find themselves. This can be shown in the case of relaxed posture when a person is in a non-threatening condition, and when under stress, the way one's body tightens or becomes rigid.

Gestures

Maneuvers can be made with hands, arms, or body, and also include head, face, and eye movements such as winking, smiling, or rolling one's eyes. Though the study of gesture is still in its infancy, researchers have established some broad categories of gestures. The so-called emblems or quotable expressions are the familiars. These are conventional, culture-specific gestures that can be used as a replacement for words, like the hand wave used for "hello" and "goodbye" in western cultures. In different cultural contexts, a single emblematic gesture can be of very different significance, ranging from complimentary to highly offensive. There are specific everyday movements like a shrug in the shoulder.

Gestures can also be categorized as being independent of speech or related to address. Speech-independent gestures rely on the understanding that is culturally acceptable and has a direct verbal translation. Examples of speech-independent expressions are a wave or a peace sign. Speech-related gestures are used in conjunction with oral speech; to reinforce the meaning being conveyed, this type of nonverbal communication is used. Speech-related movements are designed to complement a verbal message with details such as pointing to a topic of discussion.

More than anything, the facial expressions serve as a realistic means of communication. Human faces are known to be capable of more than ten thousand different emotions, with all the different muscles that specifically regulate mouth, lips, eyes, nose, forehead, and jaw. This versatility makes facial non-verbal's extremely efficient and honest unless manipulated deliberately. Furthermore, many of these emotions are universally recognized, including joy, sorrow, rage, fear, disappointment, disgust, shame, anguish, and interest.

7.3 Common Facial Signals for different Emotions

* **Happiness**

Happiness is an elusive and electrifying state. It has long sought to be established by philosophers, theologians, psychologists, and even economists. And a whole branch of psychology –positive psychology–has been dedicated to pinning it down since the 1990s. More than just a positive mood, happiness is a wellness condition that involves leading a good life, one with a sense of meaning and deep contentment. Feeling happy has its health benefits, too. A growing body of research also suggests that happiness can improve your physical health; feelings of positive and fulfillment, among other things, seem to benefit cardiovascular health, the immune system, levels of inflammation, and blood pressure. Happiness has even been associated with a longer lifespan and a higher quality of life and well-being. Achieving satisfaction is a priority worldwide. Researchers find it more important for people from every corner of the world to score satisfaction than other desirable personal outcomes, such as gaining money, receiving material goods, and entering heaven.

- **Sadness**

Sadness is an emotional pain associated with or characterized by disadvantageous emotions, loss, sadness, grief, helplessness, frustration, and sorrow. A person who experiences depression can become quiet or lethargic, and withdraw from others. Depression is an indication of extreme depression, a condition that may be brought on by major depressive disorder or chronic depressive disorder. Crying may signify sorrow. There's almost an instinctive desire to stop disappointment. We've been trying to avoid sad feelings right from a very young age. As adults, we're quick to shush wailing babies or tell the sobbing kids offhandedly, "Don't be sad! Cheer it up. You are all well. Stop crying. "They continue to pass on the message that grief is terrible and should be stopped even if not deliberate. Yet research has shown that, with real benefits, sadness can be an adaptive emotion.

- **Anxiety**

"Emotion marked by feelings of stress, worried thoughts, and physical changes such as increased blood pressure." When a person experiences potentially harmful or alarming stimuli, feelings of anxiety are not just natural but necessary for survival. The detection of predators and the emerging threat has been setting off alarms in the body since humanity's earliest days and allows for evasive action. Such warnings become evident in the form of accelerated breathing, sweating, and increased ambient sensitivity.

- **Fear**

Fear is an emotion induced by perceived danger or threat, which causes changes in physiology and ultimately, changes in behavior, such as fleeing, hiding, or freezing from recognized traumatic events. Fear in humans may occur in response to a particular danger that arises in the present or in anticipation or expectation of a future threat that is viewed as a risk to itself. The fear response stems from the sense of danger leading to a confrontation with or escapes from / evicting the threat (also known as the fight-or-flight response), which can be a freeze response or paralysis in extreme cases of fear (horror and terror). For humans and animals, the thought and learning process modulates anxiety. Therefore fear is considered rational or necessary and irrational or unacceptable. A Phobia is regarded as an unreasonable fear.

- **Anger**

Anger is an emotion characterized by antagonism towards someone or something that you feel has done you wrong intentionally. Anger can be pretty good. For example, it can give you a way to express negative feelings, or inspire you to come up with solutions to problems. Yet unnecessary wrath can cause trouble. Increased blood pressure and other anger-related physical changes make it difficult to think straight and harm your physical and mental health.

Chapter 8: Art of Faking Body Language

Is body language a "learnable skill" so can it be faked? The answer to that is yes and no. One can learn the vast majority of the more common body language. For instance, holding your hands out of your pockets or expressively using your hands to stay honest and open, or keeping your hands away from the face to come off as confident as quickly learned by conscious thinking and repetition.

Nonetheless, a new area of the study shows that there is a whole new set of signs which are much more difficult, if not impossible, to monitor. These are known as micro-expression or micro signals. Such symptoms may be used to detect truth-teller liars. Micro-expressions manifest as furrows, smirks, frowns, smiles and wrinkles and can provide an emotionally precise, but brief, window. Such micro-expressions are regulated by muscles like frontalis, corrugator, and risorius and triggered by underlying emotions that are almost impossible to monitor actively. One of those emotions is the fake smile of showing appeasement rather than genuine happiness or joy. As you will see later, the fake smile is evident, because the lips are pulled across the mouth, but the muscles that handle the eyes contribute no part.

Scientists have been able to detect such signals with advanced computer software. Computers were employed because, in fractions of seconds, the signals pulse across the face making it difficult for humans to pick up the signals actively. It can also be used to track the gestures by slowing down footage on high-speed video cameras and constantly replaying this back to observers. So part of the story is that micro-expressions are hard to detect and monitor, but the remaining story informs us that if they exist (and do), the ability to read and detect them has developed at some point.

Therefore, we have to be careful to presume that just because they happen so quickly, they can't be picked up, and conversely, we can easily fake our way through the nonverbal web. It might just be that the subconscious intuition is hard at work, giving us that sixth sense feeling that despite not being able to put words to words, can't trust anyone. The explanation, it would seem, is a mixture of micro-expressions and intuition. Many researchers are going to tell us that the face is the most natural part of our bodies to monitor, but this is not entirely true and is a poor excuse for the whole story. If our faces were managed so quickly, why do Botox procedures congeal our faces with low-level toxins to remove wrinkles? Why not simply stop using the muscles entirely and thus prevent facial wrinkles during the aging process? The simple answer is, it's not the simple one. Although our faces are, in essence, under our influence to a large extent, we cannot always focus on them, lest we can concentrate on anything else. Another way of detecting a fake is about incongruous body language. That is a language that is either incompatible with the words that are spoken and the nonverbal communication that surrounds them.

8.1 Techniques to Fake Body Language

Body language can make a deal, or break it. Even though it is hard, faking your body language will give you the result you want from any social interaction. It can motivate you to land your dream job or, when introducing your idea to your teacher, it can seem genuinely optimistic. From changing your body language to getting dressed in a way that will make you feel good. Fake it till you make it "–the idea that it will become a self-fulfilling prophecy if you behave with more confidence than you believe –is commonly suggested as a way to boost self-esteem.

Adjust the body Language

Adjusting your stance just a little so that you can make yourself bigger rather than smaller will change the way your life unfolds dramatically. The way our bodies are placed interacts with others, and with ourselves. Essentially, if we stand as champions, we behave like winners, "Emerson says. Our favorable biology gives our brain positive messages, so be tall and proud if you can.

Consider the Tone of Voice

Speaking quietly, not saying much, or hesitating while all of you are talking betrays a lack of trust. Film yourself thinking about your voice to get over your self-consciousness. "This often takes a few backs to play," she says. "And ask yourself how the way you speak may be changing. That often involves slowing down between sentences and breathing. The more you can relax and be yourself with your voice, the better you'll come across. "Anne Walsh, the vocal coach at Confidently Speaking, says," through fear and tension, we breathe high into our upper chest areas during stressful times like interviews or presentations, and this interferes with our ability to connect breathing to speak effectively. Walsh adds: "These methods are easy to learn, and can be frequently practiced until they feel natural. Relaxed, open body posture, deep, easy breathing, and a soft, resonant vocal tone build confidence. For some of us, these are not necessarily natural states, but they can be learned, practiced, and applied consciously in situations that count.

Eye Contact

In our eyes, there is over 70 percent of our sensory receptors. All the senses are dominated by the eyes-they are far more potent than all the other reasons put together. So when you're looking at people in the eye, they're forced to look at you and delegate everything else to that relation. Your eyes can not stop them. If you're in a manager meeting, maintain your eye contact with her, and she'll be less likely to look away or be distracted.
Similarly, while interacting at a team meeting, make one-on-one eye contact with each room member. As you do so, the entire room can feel your gaze's strength and be focused on you. That room power can give you a supremely, confident person's aura.

Words Articulation

All of us have heard speakers devalue what they mean by slurring over words. When you put the effort and strength behind your words, you'll sound more confident. Speak so that your audience understands every single word you give. Mumbling will make you come across as an anxious and unwilling to fully put yourself in what you say. The key to sufficient articulation is not to let the strength fall off at word ends, or sentence ends. Stay with your thoughts, and let them fully resonate with your audience.

Stay Still

If you have lots of busy gestures or flyaway movements, confusion, nervousness, anxiety, or lack of preparedness are likely to be projecting. So stop brief motions of your eyes, energetic gestures of the arm, and slight gestures of the hand, movements of the legs, or nerve twitches. Like fixing your makeup, avoid touching yourself and grooming motions too. By preceding such random or nervous gestures, you'll make every movement count and let the public see your confidence and poise.

Stand Tall

You will create a heightened image of yourself (literally!) if you sit down and stand up straight, and you will look confident no matter what you feel inside. You will also tend to be in the "up" position–ready to talk, react, and contribute to the discussion with confidence. In comparison, you can seem less concentrated and less confident if you look down, slouch or twist your body. If you have a choice between sitting and standing, then choose standing. If you give a presentation to a room full of people, or when you're on a conference call, standing up won't just inspire those in the audience, it'll also bring more strength into your speech.

8.2 The Art of Lying

Not everybody of course agrees that some lying is needed. Generations of thinkers have associated themselves with that outlook. Those who practice deceit are not only humans. Various kinds of trickery and deception were also observed in higher mammals, especially primates. The neocortex— the part of the brain that recently evolved — is essential to that capacity. The volume determines to what degree different primates can trick and manipulate, as shown in 2004 by primatologist Richard Byrne of St. Andrews University in Scotland. Current thinking about the psychological processes involved in deceit suggests that people usually tell the truth more readily than they say a lie, and that lying takes far more cognitive resources. First, we need to become aware of the truth; then we need to concoct a plausible, coherent explanation that does not contradict the observable facts. At the same time, we have to suppress the truth so we don't spill the beans— that is, we need to indulge in inhibition of the answer. What's more, we need to be able to evaluate the listener's reactions correctly so that we can deftly create changes to our original storyline if necessary. And there's the ethical aspect where we need to make a conscious decision to go beyond a social norm. All of this decision-making and self-control means deception is controlled by the prefrontal cortex— the area at the front of the brain is responsible for executive control, which involves mechanisms such as planning and managing emotions and behavior.

Also, our lies have their reasons: defending us, or protecting others while loving them. The evidence of that is that we spin stories more often for "good cause" than sheer egoism. Yet how do you become a virtuoso of this form of subtle philanthropy?

We send you some ideas... assuming, of course, that you do not usually blush when telling tales.

Keep Head up

There's always that moment in all shows when the magician threats are found, "says Jacques H. Paget*, an illusionist and specialist in negotiations. For example, when he' disappears' a ball as it remains hidden in his other hand, he may continue to turn his head to the side, a gesture that the audience may unintentionally interpret as a sign of cheating, however low. "This is a mechanical act that we all do to apologize to our conversation partner when we are afraid of being caught. Conclusion: If you are tempted to embellish your work experience during a job interview, keep the head straight. That will keep the other person from becoming suspicious.

Use the Phone

Lying over the phone is sometimes a lot simpler. "Don't expect me to have lunch with your mother, I'm still in the dentist's room," "I'm going through a tunnel, I don't have a signal..." It's natural. You can conjure up stories without even having to control your mood, reflexes, or inquisitive look. The only downside: "we have to be able to control our voices," Claudine Biland warns*. The delights of deceit cause our voices to drop a pitch to sound more calm and confident, but lying also leads us to three negative emotions— fear of being caught, shame and guilt— that can only manifest in our voices. "Besides, a British telephone insurance company has recently been tracking insurance claims for fraud through a voice analyzer. On the discovery of unusual modulations, an investigation is launched.

Repeat the Scenario

If you are telling a story, you must first incorporate it as a full role for the stage. "Actress doesn't just mean learning words. You need to be at one with your thoughts and emotions, too. These are the aspects that will usually represent your words. Playing your part with honesty, believing what you're doing, and putting yourself in your heroine's shoes is the best way to give your character more credibility.

Control the Actions

The body speaks its language and never lies, "says Dr. David J. Lieberman*, a psychology hypnotherapist, and specialist. If you're not careful, those small gestures just end up betraying you.

You sputter - your face is shivering and cracking as you announce how much you love the present you just received.

You touch your face - scratch your hair, put the finger on your mouth, rub your eyes or nose to explain your response to the delay.
Your face, your hands, your arms late, and somewhat mechanically punctuate your sentences.
Instead of a smile, you show a grimace when sharing your excitement at learning to help a colleague.
You pull your abdomen against a folder, a book, and a computer as if it were a shield. Not knowing why your partner says your statement was wrong.

Don't Say Too Much

It's the third time you call a friend to postpone lunch. She starts to find something odd when listening to you delivering your well-oiled theories, there's just too much evidence. To avoid being caught, you think it's better to increase the size of your tale: the larger it is, the more plausible it appears. It cannot possibly be invented because of its size. Your neighbor has just performed in tears at your door with his little cat's mangled body, dead in his arms... how might that be fake?

8.3 Avoiding Mistakes

Lies come in every form, size, and color. (Have you ever heard of flat-out, juvenile or white lies?) The impact of lies on beneficiaries is as diverse as individuals can be. For the liar, the minimum consequence is most likely tension. In this post, instead of a more extreme lying disorder that requires professional psychiatric intervention, we're concentrating on the "innocent, daily lies" people say. What's surprising is why people are lying (or choosing not to speak truthfully) on an ongoing basis-especially when there are communication tools that allow each of us to be fair, truthful, and courteous.

Some of the causes people choose to lie include the desire to: avoid conflict, avoid the rage or hurt of someone else, avoid hurting the feelings of someone else, decrease someone else or make them feel bad, feel more worthy of admiration and respect, gain power, avoid facing an unpleasant truth about themselves, avoid mistakes, and prevent "the boat from rocking"

Ironically, the motive behind telling a lie may be well-meaning at times, but vanity or self-centeredness is often at heart. Nevertheless, it's how the intention is implemented that's inappropriate, or that results in a strained relationship and an attitude of high stress. Can you be frank in these cases, skillfully? Sometimes, yes, and yet it takes work and diligent, consistent practice. We suggest the following exercises and strategies to help break any habit of avoiding the truth you have developed, enabling you to choose to connect respectfully and authentically.

When a person lies, it's a decision he or she made as to how to handle the situation; if a person is not mentally ill, lying is a choice sometimes made out of a lack of ability. Recognize the power-and outcome-of this self-will and those decisions if you have not already. The first course of action for skillful integrity is to change the attitude towards people who have created a habit of lying. Lying is often a "survival mode" created in adolescence or early life, so it takes the care, gentleness, and perseverance required to deconstruct a destructive habit and replace it with a safer, more skillful one.

Conclusion - Part 2

Analyzing people is an important part while communicating with other. Every person possesses different characteristics and traits. By knowing few communication skills as mentioned in this book and few personality types, we can learn how to analyze people and it will be helpful while communicating with them. Communication types may include verbal and nonverbal communication. They are necessary part when communicating with others. All types of verbal communication are speeches, presentations, and announcements, as well as casual conversations between friends. Nonverbal communication refers to gestures, facial expressions, voice tone, eye contact (or lack thereof), body language, posture, and other ways in which people can communicate without the use of words. In everyday situations like attracting a partner or in a business interview, nonverbal communication confirms a first impression: impressions are created on average within the first four seconds of interaction. First experiences or interactions with another person have a substantial impact on the understanding of an individual. As mentioned above, postures, gestures all are very important parts of nonverbal communication. After communication types, facial expressions plays very important role while analyzing people. Facial expressions like happy, sadness, angry, anxious can tell if the person we are communicating with is going through what sort of thoughts. So that we should interact with him accordingly. Personality traits plays vital role in analyzing people. Mentioned above, Myer's Brigg traits and Big five personality traits are most important ones. If you want to analyze someone perfectly, understands these traits and then communicate accordingly. Emotional Intelligence can also let you know about others true feelings. By the help of EI, you are able to understand your true feelings as well as others true feelings. So in order to analyze someone perfectly, firstly you should be aware of your emotions and then analyze others emotions.

References

Well+Good. (2020). *The dark triad personality includes narcissism, psychopathy, and a third lesser-known demonic trait.* [online] Available at: **https://www.wellandgood.com/good-advice/what-is-machiave llianism/**.

UniversalClass.com. (2020). *Various Types of Persuasion.* [online] Available at: **https://www.universalclass.com/articles/writing/various-types -of-persuasion.htm**.

Live Bold and Bloom. (2020). *How To Recognize The 8 Signs Of Emotional Manipulation.* [online] Available at: **https://liveboldandbloom.com/02/relationships/emotional-ma nipulation**.

Advancedhumanpsychology.com. (2020). *Dark Psychology – Advanced Human Psychology.* [online] Available at: **https://advancedhumanpsychology.com/category/dark-psycho logy/**.

Healthline. (2020). *15+ Signs of Emotion Manipulation.* [online] Available at: **https://www.healthline.com/health/mental-health/emotional-** manipulation#outlook.

Healthline. (2020). *Psychopath: Meaning, Signs, and vs. Sociopath.* [online] Available at: **https://www.healthline.com/health/psychopath#takeaway**.

Today, P. (2020). *Changing behaviour with neuro-linguistic programming - Personnel Today.* [online] Personnel Today. Available at:

https://www.personneltoday.com/hr/changing-behaviour-with-neuro-linguistic-programming/.

Personality - Trait theories. (2020). Retrieved 2020, from https://www.britannica.com/topic/personality/Trait-theories

The Importance of Emotional Intelligence (Including EI Quotes). (2020). Retrieved 2020, from https://positivepsychology.com/importance-of-emotional-intelligence/

How to analyze people. (2020). Retrieved 2020, from https://hubpages.com/education/How-to-analyze-people

Explainer: how we understand people and why it's important. (2020). Retrieved 2020, from https://theconversation.com/explainer-how-we-understand-people-and-why-its-important-26897

Why is it important to understand personality? (2020). Retrieved 2020, from https://preludecharacteranalysis.com/blog/why-is-it-important-to-understand-personality

Mendoza, D., Mendoza, D., & profile, V. (2020). The Importance Of Being Able To See A Situation From Another Person's Point Of View. Retrieved 2020, from http://danamendoza.blogspot.com/2011/11/importance-of-being-able-to-see.html

Benefits of the Psychology of Personality. (2020). Retrieved 2020, from https://www.ukessays.com/essays/psychology/benefits-psychology-personality-3099.php

How to Read Body Language - Revealing Secrets Behind Nonverbal Cues. (2020). Retrieved 2020, from https://fremont.edu/how-to-read-body-language-revealing-the-secrets-behind-common-nonverbal-cues/

Parvez, H., & Parvez, H. (2020). Body language: Positive and negative evaluation gestures. Retrieved February 2020, from https://www.psychmechanics.com/positive-and-negative-evaluation/